THE MARLEY COFFEE COOKBOOK

"Chef Max is passionate about food, seeing it differently than anyone and happily sharing it with everyone. If you ever have the chance to taste anything prepared by Chef Max, you know that he is gifted."

—MARGARETTE PURVIS, President & CEO Food Bank For New York City

Brimming with creative inspiration, how-to projects, and useful information to enrich your everyday life, Quarto Knows is a favorite destination for those pursuing their interests and passions. Visit our site and dig deeper with our books into your area of interest: Quarto Creates, Quarto Cooks, Quarto Homes, Quarto Lives, Quarto Drives, Quarto Explores, Quarto Gifts, or Quarto Kids.

First Published in 2017 by Quarry Books, an imprint of The Quarto Group,
100 Cummings Center, Suite 265-D, Beverly, MA 01915, USA.
T (978) 282-9590 F (978) 283-2742 QuartoKnows.com

Quarry Books titles are also available at discount for retail, wholesale, promotional, and bulk purchase. For details, contact the Special Sales Manager by email at specialsales@quarto.com or by mail at The Quarto Group, Attn: Special Sales Manager, 401 Second Avenue North, Suite 310, Minneapolis, MN 55401, USA.

10 9 8 7 6 5 4 3 2

ISBN: 978-1-63159-311-6

Digital edition published in 2017

Library of Congress Cataloging-in-Publication Data available

Design: Sussner Design Company
Page Layout: Megan Jones Design
Photography: Am Media Group LLC / Americk Lewis Nicholas Sosin Ionut Vacar, except for page 11, which is published with permission from Lindsay Oliver Donald, and images by Shutterstock on pages 26, 60, 102, 126, 176

Printed in China

THE MARLEY COFFEE COOKBOOK

ONE LOVE, MANY COFFEES
& 100 RECIPES

ROHAN MARLEY *and* MAXCEL HARDY III
with ROSEMARY BLACK

QUARRY

LIVE-CATIONS

I would like to honor everyone who has helped me in the process of building the Marley Coffee brand, believed in my vision, and helped me live it through. To my amazing family, I love you all. My Big Bro and my Big Sis, you all inspire me and keep me striving for greatness. To my kids, wow, you all are amazing. I love you so much. "Much Respect."

—ROHAN MARLEY

When reflecting on my past thirteen years as a chef, friend, family guy, and father I never would have thought I would be writing a dedication page for my second book, but God has truly blessed me. I would like to dedicate this book to everyone who believed in my crazy ideas, dreams, and goals. I would like to dedicate this book to my wonderful daughters, Tenara and Dejanae. You girls make me push harder each and every day and I'm grateful for you both.

—MAXCEL HARDY III

For my family—I can count on each of you to make me smile every day.

—ROSEMARY BLACK

CONTENTS

Preface

MY FATHER, BOB MARLEY, CAME FROM THE FARM-LANDS IN NINE MILE, JAMAICA, AND ALTHOUGH MAKING MUSIC WAS WHAT HE DID, HE DREAMED OF, ONE DAY, RETURNING TO HIS ROOTS AND BECOMING A FARMER. THAT DREAM NEVER CAME TRUE FOR HIM, BUT I WAS LUCKY ENOUGH TO TAKE HIS VISION AND MAKE IT MY OWN. I'M LUCKY ENOUGH TO BE A COFFEE GROWER, AND TO HAVE A COMPANY THAT PRODUCES ETHICALLY FARMED, ARTISAN-ROASTED COFFEE OF THE HIGHEST QUALITY.

I feel coffee came into my life for a purpose: not just so I could create more opportunities for my family and myself, but to help the communities that depend on coffee for their lives. Growing coffee is a way I can help others sustain themselves in life. It's a way for me to give back to the community and to create jobs. For me, coffee is a way to make a better tomorrow.

I didn't always think of coffee as a vehicle for sustainability, the way I do now. I'd left my homeland, Jamaica, in 1984, at the age of twelve when my family moved to the United States. During my college years, studying sociology at the University of Miami, I played football as a linebacker for the Hurricanes. While I wasn't as musical as Ziggy and some of my other siblings, I was actually a pretty good athlete. Good enough to play for one year as a professional in the Canadian Football League for the Ottawa Rough Riders (known today as the RedBlacks).

But, in my twenties, I began to dream of getting back to my roots and becoming a farmer. My father and I had shared a deep respect for nature and for all humanity. Like him, I found myself drawn to the land. In 1999, I had the opportunity to buy fifty-two acres of land in Chepstowe, in Portland, Jamaica. This area, atop Jamaica's Blue Mountains, is arguably one of the world's premier coffee-producing regions and is known for its excellent coffee-growing climate. Moisture-laden northeast trade winds reach the coastal area of Portland, Jamaica, first, and rise up the slopes of the Blue Mountains. The cool mist that blankets the area helps coffee berries ripen, yielding a fantastic aroma and flavor.

It's not just the climate that's idyllic. I learned that everything else about this area—the soils, the geology, and the vegetation of these mountains—is ideal for growing coffee.

As I walked the land I had just bought, the idea of growing coffee became my goal. I grew passionate and committed to producing the best coffee in the world. Still, it took another eight years—and plenty of red tape—before Marley Coffee finally began to flourish and grow. Today we produce sustainably grown, ethically farmed, and artisan-roasted premium coffee beans from select locations around the world, including Jamaica, Ethiopia, and Central and South America. What these climates have in common are optimal growing conditions for arabica beans—a type of coffee bean famous for its high-quality flavor and sweet aromas. Arabica beans are what all Marley coffee roasts are derived from.

Starting out, I had a lot to learn about coffee. It took time, but now I know the best coffee cherries grow under organic banana, mango, Inga, and other shade trees. And weed control can be taken care of by hand. In short, I've learned more than I could ever have imagined about growing coffee. And every day, I discover something new.

Yet while I've absorbed more coffee knowledge than I'd ever thought possible, the idea of using my coffee in recipes never occurred to me—until three years ago, when I met Chef Max Hardy through a mutual friend, Amar'e Stoudemire, the star basketball player.

Max, a personal chef who's often hired by celebrities to cook for their dinner parties, has a reputation for being generally awesome, and so, one night, I invited him to my New York City apartment to cook for some friends and me. When Max arrived at my apartment and saw all the bags of freshly ground coffee in my kitchen, he asked if he could use some in his cooking. That night he whipped up this great coffee-infused syrup, along with some of his crazy good fried chicken and waffles. My friends went wild for this dish, especially the syrup, and so did I. The next day, when I realized all the chicken, waffles, and syrup were gone, I called Max and asked him to come back to my apartment and make the dish again.

One dish led to the next, and, pretty soon, we were having so much fun cooking and eating the dishes made with various types of coffee, we realized we were onto something big: using coffee as an essential ingredient in a wide variety of dishes. Not just brewed coffee, but the beans, finely ground, too. In our minds and in my kitchen, coffee had become not just something to drink, but a magical ingredient to flavor, enhance, and enliven food. Sharing the story of coffee, as well as our favorite dishes made with coffee, is what we are passionate about. It's why we decided to write this book. One love, and many coffees, and a rich assortment of dishes you'll treasure, each made with coffee.

Introduction

COFFEE ROCKS THE WORLD—AND THE WORLD LOVES COFFEE RIGHT BACK. IT'S THE DAILY BREW OF MILLIONS WHO DRINK IT TO FEEL ENERGIZED, FOCUSED, AND FUELED FOR THE DAY AHEAD. WE START AND, VERY OFTEN, END OUR DAY WITH COFFEE. WHETHER IT'S ENJOYED LIGHT AND SWEET OR BLACK, FROTHED OR FOAMED, ICED OR STEAMING, COFFEE IS THE BEVERAGE OF CHOICE GLOBALLY. SOME 500 BILLION CUPS OF COFFEE ARE CONSUMED ANNUALLY AROUND THE WORLD.

Photo courtesy of Lindsay Oliver Donald

Coffee is truly an intellectual beverage. It speaks to everyone, from those who jump-start their day with a mugful to those who see it as a reason for socializing. As we discovered when we started to cook together, coffee can transform a dish into something really special. With its multifaceted, nuanced flavor profile, coffee may just be the perfect ingredient. Coffee can make a dish sing, and its multitude of subtle notes means that it blends well across the board with everything from sugar to spices to salt. Coffee, more complex than wine, can be subtle and muted, have overtones of nutmeg and other spices, or possess exotic floral notes. Some coffees are known for their rich, dark chocolaty finish; others for their smooth, light, and smoky taste. Depending upon its flavor, a particular coffee might lend itself to mellowing out a sauce, or firing up the flavor in steak or chicken, or taking a dessert to a completely new level of decadence. Deciding how to pair coffees with other ingredients in recipes has resulted in an amazing and magical journey for us. The collection we've put our heads together to create is really memorable.

When we were creating recipes, whether we wanted to eat traditional Jamaican fare, or a dish from the Bahamas, which is where Max's family comes from, or from the U.S., where we both live, we came to discover that coffee would give it that extra flavor kick. And so we added it to main courses (a savory jalapeño and coffee–infused gumbo, a coconut curry root vegetable stew, coffee-grilled lamb chops) and sweets—apple bread pudding, chocolate lava cakes, and Key lime pie. We added it to rubs and spice blends, syrups and salads and sides, and vegetables of all kinds.

At the heart of each recipe is Marley Coffee, which is like no other. At Marley Coffee, we use no chemical pesticides, herbicides, fertilizers, or other additives. Instead, sustainable and organic farming practices are employed on our biodiverse farm, which is designed to help preserve Earth's natural balance. But, while we created these recipes using Marley Coffee, that certainly doesn't mean they aren't as delicious made with other coffees.

As you cook your way through these pages, we hope you will use whatever kind of coffee you love and rely on. We hope, too, that you will feel comfortable being flexible and creative when cooking from this book. The best recipes are those you adapt and tailor to fit your own preferences. This book is meant as a guide, not a set-in-stone cookbook. We want you to personalize these dishes so they are your very own. And, as you cook, you will come to realize how comfortably and perfectly coffee goes with food, wherever in the world you call home.

Every cup of coffee tells a story. And in this book, we share with you the story of Marley Coffee and our personal collection of the best recipes this coffee has inspired.

CHAPTER

1

ALL THE ESSENTIALS

Coffee is one of those things nearly everyone consumes daily. It's kind of like music: When it's top-notch quality, it's inspiring. It makes you happy, and it moves you. It has a place in just about every meal. But its strong role in basic recipes, whether as a marinade, vinaigrette, or spice blend, is essential for cooks who are looking to elevate their cooking from ordinary to exceptional. Just a little coffee, whether some very finely ground beans or a splash of brewed java, lends body and balance to innumerable dishes. The essentials in this chapter are the building blocks of our coffee-inspired recipe collection.

Here, you'll find recipes to make again and again, like the Marley Coffee Spice Blend (page 14), which brightens just about every type of meat or vegetable you can think of, and sauces that lend depth to a variety of dishes and also serve as lively marinades for chicken, fish, and meat.

Here, too, is where you'll turn when you want a special salad dressing. This chapter has coffee-infused vinaigrettes that transform a salad from simple to superior. Explore this chapter, and think of it as an introduction to cooking with coffee and as a foundation for the recipes you will find later in the book.

MARLEY COFFEE SPICE BLEND

YIELD: ⅔ CUP (ABOUT 73 G)

Every cook needs a quintessential spice blend—one that enlivens rubs, marinades, dressings, and omelets. This blend, redolent of onion and curry, as well as one of the world's finest coffees—Jamaican Blue Mountain coffee—fills the bill perfectly. Blue Mountain coffee is rich, full-bodied, and perfectly balanced, and it possesses a seductive floral aroma. Its complex notes make it the perfect complement to assertive spices like anise and garlic, and its aroma makes it invaluable as an ingredient in a rub. Truly the essential spice blend for the recipes in this book, it will keep for a couple of months at room temperature. Store it in a Mason jar and use it with meats and poultry, eggs, vinaigrettes, and even heartier fish dishes.

INGREDIENTS

2 TABLESPOONS VERY FINELY GROUND TALKIN' BLUES COFFEE BEANS

2 TABLESPOONS GROUND ANISE

2 TABLESPOONS ONION POWDER

1 TABLESPOON GROUND CUMIN

1 TABLESPOON PACKED LIGHT BROWN SUGAR

1 TABLESPOON DRIED, GROUND THYME

1 TEASPOON CURRY POWDER

1 TEASPOON KOSHER SALT

½ TEASPOON CAYENNE PEPPER

½ TEASPOON GROUND NUTMEG

½ TEASPOON GROUND ALLSPICE

DIRECTIONS

In a medium-size bowl, stir together all the ingredients until well mixed. Transfer the mixture to a Mason jar or other container with a tight-fitting lid. Cover and store in a cool, dry place for up to 2 months.

NOTE: Anise, also known as aniseed or anise seed, flavors a variety of sweet and savory dishes. Typically, it's not as widely used as, say, cumin or curry powder. But don't let that bottle of anise languish on your spice rack. Use it to flavor sweet and savory breads as well as vegetables such as cabbage, carrots, and cucumbers.

COFFEE-SPICED BARBECUE SAUCE

YIELD: ABOUT 2 ½ CUPS (ABOUT 625 G)

If coffee strikes you as an unusual ingredient in a barbecue sauce, be advised that when simmered with apple cider vinegar, ketchup, agave nectar, and a generous infusion of dry mustard, its flavor becomes multifaceted. Unquestionably one of our favorites to grab when marinating meat or poultry, this flavorful sauce is infused with brewed Lively Up! coffee, one of the richest-bodied, darkest, and boldest of the Marley coffees. Thanks to its balanced acidity, this wonderful barbecue sauce deepens the flavor of not just meats and poultry destined for the grill, but roasted and baked dishes as well.

INGREDIENTS

2 CUPS (480 G) KETCHUP

½ CUP (120 ML) APPLE CIDER VINEGAR

¼ CUP (60 ML) AGAVE NECTAR

¼ CUP (60 ML) BREWED LIVELY UP! COFFEE

¼ CUP (60 ML) HOT SAUCE, OR TO TASTE

3 TABLESPOONS (60 G) MOLASSES

JUICE OF 1 LIME

1 TABLESPOON DRY MUSTARD

1 CLOVE GARLIC, MINCED

½ TEASPOON LIQUID SMOKE

PINCH KOSHER SALT

DIRECTIONS

In a medium-size saucepan over medium heat, stir together the ketchup, cider vinegar, agave nectar, coffee, hot sauce, molasses, lime juice, dry mustard, garlic, liquid smoke, and salt. Bring to a boil. Reduce the heat to low and cook for 5 minutes, or until the sauce is thick and smooth.

When the sauce has cooled slightly, transfer it to a container. Cover tightly and refrigerate.

TIP: KEEP THIS REFRIGERATED AND USE WITHIN A COUPLE OF WEEKS.

❧ JERK SEASONING ❧

YIELD: 2 CUPS (ABOUT 455 G)

The quintessential seasoning mix for chicken, this is also great on seafood, or even in a vinaigrette. With the addition of brewed Buffalo Soldier coffee, this seasoning mix makes the best jerk chicken you'll ever taste.

INGREDIENTS

3 SCALLIONS (WHITE AND LIGHT GREEN PARTS), SLICED THIN

1 CUP (175 G) DICED FRESH MANGO

½ YELLOW ONION, CUT INTO ½-INCH (1 CM) CHUNKS

6 CLOVES GARLIC, PEELED

2 TABLESPOONS (30 ML) EXTRA-VIRGIN OLIVE OIL

2 TABLESPOONS (40 G) HONEY

2 TABLESPOONS (30 ML) LOW-SODIUM SOY SAUCE

2 TABLESPOONS (30 G) PACKED DARK BROWN SUGAR

2 TABLESPOONS MINCED FRESH GINGER

2 SPRIGS FRESH THYME, STEMMED

1 TABLESPOON GROUND CINNAMON

1 TABLESPOON GROUND ALLSPICE

1 TABLESPOON GROUND NUTMEG

1 TABLESPOON GROUND WHITE PEPPER

1 SCOTCH BONNET PEPPER, CHOPPED

¼ CUP (60 ML) BREWED, COOLED BUFFALO SOLDIER COFFEE

DIRECTIONS

In the work bowl of a food processor, combine the scallions, mango, onion, garlic, olive oil, honey, soy sauce, brown sugar, ginger, thyme, cinnamon, allspice, nutmeg, white pepper, Scotch bonnet pepper, and coffee. Pulse until the mixture is well blended. Transfer the seasoning mix to a Mason jar, cover tightly, and keep refrigerated.

TIP: STORED IN THE REFRIGERATOR, THIS WILL LAST FOR UP TO 1 WEEK.

I WAS ALWAYS INTERESTED IN FARMING. AS A CHILD, I HAD A LOT OF DAILY CHORES TO DO, LIKE WEEDING THE GARDEN, WATERING THE PLANTS, GOING INTO THE CANE FIELDS OR THE MANGO BUSHES. EVERYTHING IN JAMAICA IS SORT OF FARM RELATED! WHEN I GREW UP, THAT LOVE OF FARMING JUST GREW AND GREW INSIDE ME. I KNEW I WANTED TO BE CLOSE TO THE LAND.

❖ BLACKENED SPICE ❖

YIELD: ⅓ CUP (ABOUT 25 G)

This blend of subtly sweet and spicy is the perfect seasoning for chicken and seafood. Consider making a double batch as you'll use it often.

INGREDIENTS

1 TABLESPOON PAPRIKA

2 TEASPOONS GARLIC POWDER

2 TEASPOONS ONION POWDER

2 TEASPOONS FINELY GROUND BUFFALO SOLDIER
    COFFEE BEANS

2 TEASPOONS GROUND CUMIN

2 TEASPOONS DRIED PARSLEY

2 TEASPOONS LIGHT BROWN SUGAR

2 TEASPOONS CAYENNE PEPPER

1 TEASPOON KOSHER SALT

1 TEASPOON FRESHLY GROUND BLACK PEPPER

DIRECTIONS

In a medium-size bowl, stir together the paprika, garlic powder, onion powder, ground coffee, cumin, parsley, brown sugar, cayenne, salt, and black pepper until well mixed. Transfer the spice mix to a Mason jar or other container with a tight-fitting lid.

TIP: FOR BEST RESULTS, STORE THIS IN A COOL, DRY PLACE, TIGHTLY COVERED. IT WILL LAST FOR A COUPLE OF MONTHS.

BALSAMIC-INFUSED VINAIGRETTE
❧ WITH COFFEE ❧

YIELD: ABOUT 1½ CUPS (ABOUT 355 ML)

Get Up, Stand Up coffee tempers the balsamic vinegar and rounds out the flavor in this vinaigrette. Drizzle over blackened fish and your favorite salads.

INGREDIENTS

½ CUP (120 ML) BALSAMIC VINEGAR

¼ CUP (60 ML) BREWED, COOLED GET UP, STAND UP COFFEE

¼ CUP (85 G) HONEY

2 CLOVES GARLIC, PEELED

1 SHALLOT, PEELED AND TRIMMED

2 TABLESPOONS (30 G) PACKED LIGHT BROWN SUGAR

1 TEASPOON RED PEPPER FLAKES

½ CUP (120 ML) EXTRA-VIRGIN OLIVE OIL

DIRECTIONS

In a blender, combine the vinegar, coffee, honey, garlic, shallot, brown sugar, and red pepper flakes. Purée at high speed for about 20 seconds.

With the blender running, gradually add the olive oil in a thin stream. Continue to purée the dressing for about 2 minutes, or until thick and emulsified.

TIP: THIS DRESSING WILL KEEP, TIGHTLY COVERED, FOR UP TO 3 WEEKS IN THE REFRIGERATOR.

COFFEE-INFUSED MANGO-PEPPER
❧ VINAIGRETTE ❧

YIELD: 1¼ CUPS (ABOUT 285 ML)

This lively vinaigrette turns just about any green salad into something special. The coffee provides spicy, almost fruity, notes that complement the mango and ginger. This is a very easy vinaigrette to make in a blender.

INGREDIENTS

2 RIPE MANGOS, PITTED, PEELED, AND DICED

1 RED BELL PEPPER, CORED, SEEDED, AND DICED

½ CUP (120 ML) COCONUT VINEGAR

¼ CUP (60 ML) BREWED, COOLED MYSTIC MORNING COFFEE

3 TABLESPOONS (60 G) AGAVE NECTAR

1 SHALLOT, PEELED AND TRIMMED

1 CLOVE GARLIC, PEELED

1 TEASPOON MINCED FRESH GINGER

½ CUP (120 ML) EXTRA-VIRGIN OLIVE OIL

SALT AND FRESHLY GROUND BLACK PEPPER TO TASTE

DIRECTIONS

In a blender, combine the mangos, red bell pepper, coconut vinegar, coffee, agave nectar, shallot, garlic, and ginger. Purée at high speed for 20 seconds.

With the blender running, slowly pour in the olive oil. Continue puréeing for 2 minutes, or until thick. Season the dressing with salt and pepper. Transfer to a container with a tight-fitting lid.

TIP: REFRIGERATE, TIGHTLY COVERED, FOR UP TO 1 WEEK. IN ADDITION TO DRESSING SALADS, TRY THIS VINAIGRETTE AS A MARINADE FOR FISH OR CHICKEN.

❧ COFFEE TERIYAKI SAUCE ❧

YIELD: 2 CUPS (ABOUT 475 ML)

Coffee enlivens and deepens the flavor of purchased teriyaki in this sauce, which makes a fabulously flavorful marinade.

INGREDIENTS

2 CUPS (475 ML) TERIYAKI SAUCE

¼ CUP (60 ML) BREWED, COOLED MYSTIC MORNING COFFEE

2 SHALLOTS, CHOPPED

2 SCALLIONS (WHITE AND LIGHT GREEN PARTS), CHOPPED

2 TEASPOONS (4 G) MINCED FRESH GINGER

2 CLOVES GARLIC, MASHED

DIRECTIONS

In a medium-size saucepan over medium heat, whisk the teriyaki sauce, coffee, shallots, scallions, ginger, and garlic. Bring to a boil, whisking constantly.

When the sauce boils, reduce the heat to low and let it simmer for about 10 minutes. Transfer the sauce to a food processor or blender. Pulse or blend for 30 seconds. Strain through a fine-mesh strainer, transfer to a covered container, and refrigerate.

TIP: SERVE THIS WITH YOUR FAVORITE CHICKEN, FISH, OR PORK DISH, OR TOSS SOME WITH COOKED VEGETABLES.

COFFEE AND STAR ANISE–INFUSED OIL

YIELD: 2 CUPS (436 G)

This requires a bit of planning that will be reward-ed. Start to make this a few days before you plan to use it; it takes three to five days to fully develop its delicious coffee taste. This versatile oil can be used in marinades, such as for the Grilled Vegetable Skewers Marinated in Coffee and Star Anise–Infused Oil (page 80), sauces, salad dressings—and even desserts, like the Coffee Oil–Infused Butter Cake with Blackberry Compote (page 184)—for an instant flavor boost.

INGREDIENTS

2 CUPS (436 G) COCONUT OIL

6 WHOLE BUFFALO SOLDIER COFFEE BEANS

2 STAR ANISE

DIRECTIONS

In a clean, empty wine bottle, or other glass container such as a Mason jar, combine the coconut oil, coffee beans, and star anise. Cover and set aside for several days at room temperature. The oil will have a clear brown tone to it—but not dark brown—and a fragrant, robust, coffee flavor and aroma when it's ready to use.

TIP: THIS WILL KEEP FOR A FEW WEEKS IN THE REFRIGERATOR.

❖ GUAVA SAUCE FLAVORED WITH COFFEE ❖

YIELD: 1¼ CUPS (ABOUT 285 ML)

Spoon this sweet, exotic sauce over pound cake or your favorite ice cream. It's so good you might just eat it with a spoon!

INGREDIENTS

1 CUP (235 ML) GUAVA PURÉE

¼ CUP (60 ML) BREWED, COOLED MYSTIC MORNING COFFEE

3 TABLESPOONS (45 G) PACKED LIGHT BROWN SUGAR

3 TABLESPOONS (45 ML) DARK RUM, PREFERABLY MARLEY BRAND

1 TEASPOON MINCED FRESH GINGER

DIRECTIONS

In a medium-size saucepan over medium heat, whisk the guava purée, coffee, brown sugar, rum, and ginger. Bring to a boil, whisking constantly.

When the sauce boils, reduce the heat to low and let it simmer for about 2 minutes, or until it starts to thicken.

TIP: THIS SAUCE IS DELICIOUS HOT OR COLD. REFRIGERATE IT, PREFERABLY IN AN AIRTIGHT CONTAINER WITH A LID.

CHAPTER

2

EYE-OPENING BREAKFASTS AND MORNING NIBBLES

(Mystic Morning coffee)

Millions of us start our day with a cup of coffee, and a favorite is a medium-roast coffee that is a Central American and Ethiopian blend. It certainly makes any morning seem better. Mystic Morning coffee, for instance, has overtones of nutmeg and cocoa brightened with a spicy finish. A full-bodied coffee such as this one makes the perfect enhancement to a variety of sweet and savory breakfast dishes.

Bright and vibrant, Mystic Morning gives a boost to so many dishes we associate with breakfast. For Coffee-Crusted Rib Eye Steak with Eggs (page 40), the quintessential high-protein breakfast, the meat is rubbed with a coffee-infused spice blend before being panfried in a skillet. The skillet is then deglazed with some brewed coffee. Classic, but with a twist, banana pancakes, pecan-cranberry bread, and coconut almond-crusted French toast, all benefit from the addition of coffee. Coffee also invigorates the traditional Jamaican breakfast, Coffee-Infused Ackee and Saltfish (page 36), and enhances a simple fruit compote.

Wake up to some of these coffee-enriched dishes, enjoy each and every one, and create your own riffs. It's going to be a great day!

SWEET POTATO
❧ WAFFLES ❧

YIELD: 4 OR 5 WAFFLES

These delicious waffles make a special weekend break-fast treat. Coffee lends a richness, and warm maple syrup flavored with pecans and vanilla makes an extraordinary topping. Is it Sunday yet?

INGREDIENTS

1 ½ LARGE SWEET POTATOES, PEELED AND DICED

3 EGGS

¾ CUP (175 ML) BUTTERMILK

¼ CUP (60 ML) BREWED, COOLED MYSTIC MORNING COFFEE

2 TABLESPOONS (30 ML) MELTED UNSALTED BUTTER

2 CUPS (224 G) ALL-PURPOSE FLOUR

3 TABLESPOONS (39 G) SUGAR

1 ½ TEASPOONS BAKING POWDER

1 TEASPOON GROUND CINNAMON

1 TABLESPOON (15 ML) VANILLA EXTRACT

MAPLE SYRUP, FOR SERVING (SEE TIP)

DIRECTIONS

In a small saucepan of boiling water over medium heat, cook the sweet potatoes for 10 minutes, or until soft. Drain into a colander, transfer to a plate, and mash with a fork.

Preheat a waffle iron to medium-high.

In a large bowl, whisk the eggs, buttermilk, coffee, and butter until light and foamy.

With a large spoon, stir in the flour, sugar, baking powder, cinnamon, and vanilla. Continue to stir until the batter is smooth and the dry ingredients are well incorporated into the egg and buttermilk mixture. Fold in the mashed sweet potato and mix well.

Ladle enough batter into the preheated waffle iron to make 1 waffle. Follow the manufacturer's directions for cooking the waffle. Typically, it takes about 3 minutes for a waffle to become crisp and golden. Continue with the remaining batter.

TIP: TO JAZZ UP PLAIN MAPLE SYRUP, SIMMER IT OVER LOW HEAT WITH SOME CHOPPED PECANS AND A DASH OF VANILLA EXTRACT UNTIL VERY WARM.

COCONUT-ALMOND-CRUSTED FRENCH TOAST WITH
❖ COFFEE AND RUM WHIPPED CREAM ❖

YIELD: 4 SERVINGS

When heavy cream is whipped with dark rum and a medium-roast coffee, it becomes a sublime topping. Use it on everything from a fudgy chocolate cake to a fruit tart to this unusually good challah bread French toast. What a way to wake up!

INGREDIENTS

FOR FRENCH TOAST:

6 EGGS

¾ CUP (175 ML) HALF-AND-HALF

¼ CUP (50 G) GRANULATED SUGAR

1 TEASPOON (5 ML) VANILLA EXTRACT

1 TEASPOON GROUND CINNAMON

¾ CUP (180 G) PACKED LIGHT BROWN SUGAR

1¾ CUPS (149 G) SHREDDED UNSWEETENED COCONUT

½ CUP (55 G) CHOPPED ALMONDS

¾ CUP (21 G) CRUSHED CORNFLAKES

1 LOAF CHALLAH BREAD, SLICED INTO 1-INCH-THICK (2.5 CM) SLICES

8 TABLESPOONS (1 STICK, OR 113 G) UNSALTED BUTTER, DIVIDED

½ CUP (120 ML) EXTRA-VIRGIN OLIVE OIL, DIVIDED, OR AS NEEDED

FOR WHIPPED CREAM:

½ CUP (120 ML) HEAVY WHIPPING CREAM, WELL CHILLED

3 TABLESPOONS (45 ML) BREWED, COLD MYSTIC MORNING COFFEE

3 TABLESPOONS (45 ML) DARK RUM, PREFERABLY MARLEY BRAND

3 TABLESPOONS (23 G) CONFECTIONERS' SUGAR

DIRECTIONS

TO MAKE THE FRENCH TOAST:

Preheat the oven to warm.

In a large bowl, whisk the eggs, half-and-half, granulated sugar, vanilla, and cinnamon. Set aside.

On a large plate, stir together the brown sugar, coconut, almonds, and cornflakes.

Dip the challah slices into the egg mixture and let the excess drip off. Dredge the slices in the coconut-almond mixture, turning to coat both sides.

In a large skillet over medium heat, melt 1 tablespoon butter with 1 tablespoon (15 ml) olive oil. When very hot, add the challah slices a few at a time. Cook for 2 to 3 minutes, or until golden brown on both sides, being careful not to let the coating burn. Add more butter and oil to the skillet as needed.

As the slices are done, place them on a parchment paper–lined baking sheet in the warm oven. Continue to cook the remaining slices, adding more butter and oil as needed.

TO MAKE THE WHIPPED CREAM:

In a medium-size bowl, use an electric mixer at high speed to beat the heavy cream until soft peaks form. Add the coffee, rum, and confectioners' sugar. Continue to beat until the whipped cream is thick enough to scoop out of the bowl with a spoon. Be careful not to overbeat! Serve the French toast topped with the whipped cream.

❧ COFFEE-SPICED DUMPLINGS ❧

YIELD: 10 DUMPLINGS

These small, succulent fried dumplings dress up so many dishes. We love them with Coffee-Infused Ackee and Saltfish (page 36), and they are delicious in soups. The traditional dough is spiced just enough to make the dumplings flavorful, but not so much that they overpower the taste of whatever dish you serve them with.

INGREDIENTS

3 CUPS (336 G) ALL-PURPOSE FLOUR, PLUS MORE
  FOR THE WORK SURFACE

¾ CUP (105 G) CORNMEAL

2 TABLESPOONS (26 G) SUGAR

1 TABLESPOON BAKING POWDER

1 TEASPOON MARLEY COFFEE SPICE BLEND (PAGE 14)

½ TEASPOON KOSHER SALT

2 TABLESPOONS (28 G) UNSALTED BUTTER, SOFTENED

1 CUP (235 ML) MILK

3 CUPS (705 ML) VEGETABLE OIL

DIRECTIONS

In a large bowl, stir together the flour, cornmeal, sugar, baking powder, Marley Coffee Spice Blend, and salt. With your fingertips, gradually work in the butter until it is no longer visible and the dough looks like crumbs. Pour in the milk and stir very well to combine. When a soft dough forms, transfer it to a lightly floured work surface.

Knead the dough for about 45 seconds, or until soft and pliable. Divide the dough into 10 equal pieces. Let rest for about 10 minutes.

Pour the vegetable oil into a large, heavy saucepan over medium heat and let it preheat to 350°F (180°C). Add the dumplings, a few at a time, to the hot oil. Fry them for 5 minutes, turning occasionally, or until golden brown. With tongs, transfer the dumplings from the hot oil to paper towels to drain.

TIP: THESE DUMPLINGS TASTE BEST WHEN SERVED FRESHLY MADE AND PIPING HOT.

SWEET POTATO AND ONION HASH
❧ WITH POACHED EGGS ❧

YIELD: 5 SERVINGS

A sassy riff on classic hash browns, this is a wonderful brunch dish for a group. Nestled in the savory hash that gets a lively kick from Marley Coffee Spice Blend (page 14) and an infusion of Mystic Morning coffee, the eggs feature deliciously runny yolks and firm whites.

INGREDIENTS

2 LARGE SWEET POTATOES, PEELED AND CUT INTO ½-INCH (1 CM) DICE

¼ CUP (60 ML) EXTRA-VIRGIN OLIVE OIL

1 RED BELL PEPPER, CORED, SEEDED, AND DICED

¼ ONION, DICED (ABOUT ¼ CUP, OR 40 G)

2 CLOVES GARLIC, MINCED

½ BUNCH FRESH CURLY PARSLEY, STEMMED AND CHOPPED

2 TABLESPOONS (ABOUT 24 G) MARLEY COFFEE SPICE BLEND (PAGE 14)

1 TABLESPOON CHOPPED FRESH THYME LEAVES

1 TEASPOON UNSALTED BUTTER

¼ CUP (60 ML) BREWED MYSTIC MORNING COFFEE

5 EGGS

SALT AND FRESHLY GROUND PEPPER TO TASTE

DIRECTIONS

Preheat the oven to 375°F (190°C, or gas mark 5).

Bring a 2-quart saucepan of water to a boil over high heat. Add the sweet potatoes and return the water to a boil. Reduce the heat to low and simmer the sweet potatoes, uncovered, for 4 to 6 minutes, or until they just start to soften. Drain well and set aside.

In a large, heavy, ovenproof skillet or sauté pan over medium heat, heat the olive oil for 2 minutes, or until very hot. Add the cooked sweet potato, red bell pepper, onion, garlic, parsley, Marley Coffee Spice Blend, thyme, and butter. Sauté the mixture for about 5 minutes, or until the vegetables begin to caramelize and the sweet potato starts to turn a golden brown color.

Add the coffee and simmer for 2 minutes more. With a spatula, spread the vegetable mixture evenly in the pan.

Crack the eggs over the vegetable mixture, taking care not to break the yolks. Place the pan in the oven. Bake the hash and eggs for 8 to 10 minutes, or until the egg whites are opaque and the yolks are still a bit runny. If you like your yolks on the firmer side leave the pan in the oven for another 3 minutes or so. Season with salt and pepper and serve immediately.

TIP: SERVE THIS DISH WITH YOUR FAVORITE BREAKFAST MEATS FOR AN EXTRA-HEARTY BREAKFAST.

COFFEE-INFUSED ACKEE AND SALTFISH

YIELD: 4 SERVINGS

In our version of this traditional Jamaican breakfast dish, callaloo, popular in Caribbean cooking, adds color and flavor and Mystic Morning coffee brightens and enhances the ackee.

Callaloo—the edible green leaves of the taro root—is cooked in the same manner as turnip or collard greens. If you can't find it, substitute 2 bunches fresh spinach.

Ackee, a bright red tropical fruit, when ripe, yields a soft, creamy white flesh—a must-have in this dish. You should be able to find canned ackee easily, produced by Grace Foods. Serve this robust dish with plenty of coffee!

INGREDIENTS

1 POUND (454 G) SALTFISH

2 TABLESPOONS (30 ML) EXTRA-VIRGIN OLIVE OIL

2 SCALLIONS (WHITE, LIGHT GREEN, AND DARK GREEN PARTS), CHOPPED

½ GREEN OR RED BELL PEPPER, CORED, SEEDED, AND SLICED THIN (ABOUT ½ CUP, OR 75 G)

½ LARGE, RIPE TOMATO, DICED (ABOUT ½ CUP, OR 90 G)

¼ ONION, DICED (ABOUT ¼ CUP, OR 40 G)

2 CLOVES GARLIC, MINCED

¼ SCOTCH BONNET PEPPER, SEEDED AND DICED

2 SPRIGS FRESH THYME

2 (8-OUNCE, OR 225 G) CANS ACKEE, DRAINED

1 BUNCH CALLALOO, RINSED AND TRIMMED

FRESHLY GROUND BLACK PEPPER TO TASTE

1 TABLESPOON (15 ML) FRESHLY SQUEEZED LIME JUICE, PLUS MORE TO TASTE

2 TABLESPOONS (30 ML) BREWED MYSTIC MORNING COFFEE

DIRECTIONS

In a large bowl, combine the saltfish with enough cold water to cover it. Set aside to soak for about 1 hour. Occasionally, pour off the water and rinse the saltfish under cold running water to remove as much salt as possible. After 1 hour, drain the saltfish.

Bring a large, heavy pot of water to a boil. Add the saltfish and cook for 8 to 10 minutes, or until tender and flaky. Remove the saltfish from the water and set aside briefly to cool. When cool enough to handle, check carefully for any bones; use your fingers to remove them. Flake the saltfish into bite-size chunks. Set aside.

In a large skillet or sauté pan over medium heat, heat the olive oil for 1 minute. Add the scallions, bell pepper, tomato, onion, garlic, Scotch bonnet pepper, and thyme. Sauté for about 3 minutes, or until the vegetables begin to soften.

Add the flaked saltfish, ackee, callaloo, pepper, and lime juice. Simmer for about 3 minutes, stirring occasionally. When all ingredients are well incorporated, pour in the coffee and simmer for about 1½ minutes. Taste and add additional lime juice and pepper as needed. (Thanks to the saltfish, you probably won't need salt.)

TIP: IF YOU'D LIKE TO SERVE THIS DISH WITH AN ADDITIONAL VEGETABLE, FRIED PLANTAINS ARE A GREAT OPTION. IT ALSO GOES REALLY WELL WITH COFFEE-SPICED DUMPLINGS (PAGE 33).

NOTE FROM ROHAN MARLEY

MY FATHER WASN'T A BIG COFFEE DRINKER, ALTHOUGH HE DRANK A LOT OF TEA. HE DRANK STUFF THAT I DIDN'T LIKE, SUCH AS FISH TEA, AND COLLARD SOUP, AND BEETROOT JUICE. AND I REMEMBER THAT WE ALWAYS HAD PINEAPPLE AND GINGER IN OUR HOUSE. I WILL NEVER FORGET HOW THESE SMELLED. MY FATHER LIKED HIS FRUIT JUICE. IN THE MORNING, I ALWAYS HAVE TO HAVE SOME FRUIT JUICE. COFFEE AND JUICE IS HOW I LIKE TO START MY DAY.

COFFEE-CRUSTED RIB EYE STEAK WITH EGGS

YIELD: 4 SERVINGS

The light notes that characterize Mystic Morning coffee don't overpower the flavors of the steak in this hearty breakfast offering. Instead, the steak's great flavor is nicely accentuated by the coffee. Serve with steaming mugs of freshly brewed Mystic Morning coffee and say "hello" to a new day.

INGREDIENTS

4 (8-OUNCE, OR 225 G) RIB EYE STEAKS

2 TABLESPOONS (ABOUT 24 G) MARLEY COFFEE SPICE BLEND (PAGE 14)

2 CLOVES GARLIC, MINCED

1 SPRIG FRESH ROSEMARY, LEAVES STRIPPED AND CHOPPED

2 TABLESPOONS (30 ML) EXTRA-VIRGIN OLIVE OIL, DIVIDED

¼ CUP (60 ML) BREWED MYSTIC MORNING COFFEE

4 EGGS

KOSHER SALT AND FRESHLY GROUND BLACK PEPPER TO TASTE

DIRECTIONS

Sprinkle each steak evenly with the Marley Coffee Spice Blend, garlic, rosemary, and 1 teaspoon (5 ml) olive oil.

Preheat a large cast iron skillet over medium-high heat. When the skillet is very hot, add the steaks and sear them for about 2 minutes per side. Continue to cook the steaks to your desired doneness. Depending upon the size of your skillet, you may need to cook the steaks in 2 batches. Transfer the cooked steaks to a platter and let rest at room temperature for about 3 minutes to ensure all juices are locked in.

Meanwhile, in a nonstick skillet over medium heat, heat the remaining olive oil until very hot. Crack the eggs and add them to the pan. Cook the eggs for about 3 minutes, or until the whites are cooked and the yolks are bright yellow and runny. Season with salt and pepper.

Return the cast iron skillet to medium-high heat. Carefully pour the coffee into the skillet and cook it, stirring, for 2 or 3 minutes to deglaze the pan. Pour this deglazing mixture over the steaks. Serve the steaks with the eggs.

TIP: SUBSTITUTE YOUR FAVORITE STEAK IF YOU CAN'T FIND RIB EYES. AND FOR FIRMER EGGS, LEAVE THEM IN THE PAN FOR A COUPLE MINUTES MORE.

❧ BANANA AND COFFEE–INFUSED PANCAKES ❧

YIELD: 4 SERVINGS (2 LARGE PANCAKES OR 3 SILVER DOLLAR-SIZE PANCAKES PER SERVING)

Tender and fluffy, these classic banana pancakes will become a sweet tradition in your family. An infusion of a mellow coffee heightens their banana flavor.

INGREDIENTS

2 CUPS (250 G) WHOLE-WHEAT FLOUR

2 TABLESPOONS (26 G) SUGAR

2 TEASPOONS BAKING POWDER

½ TEASPOON BAKING SODA

½ TEASPOON SALT

2 CUPS (475 ML) BUTTERMILK

2 EGGS

3 TABLESPOONS (45 ML) VEGETABLE OIL

½ CUP (112 G) MASHED BANANA
(ABOUT 1 SMALL BANANA)

¼ CUP (60 ML) BREWED, COOLED MYSTIC
MORNING COFFEE

TIP: FOR A DELICIOUS COFFEE-PECAN SYRUP TO TOP THESE PANCAKES, ADD ¼ CUP (27.5 G) CHOPPED PECANS AND ¼ CUP (60 ML) BREWED COFFEE TO 1 CUP (322 G) MAPLE SYRUP. YOU MAY KEEP THE COOKED PANCAKES WARM IN A LOOSELY COVERED PAN IN A PREHEATED, 275°F (140°C, OR GAS MARK 1) OVEN FOR UP TO 30 MINUTES. THIS RECIPE MAY BE DOUBLED TO SERVE A CROWD OF HUNGRY PANCAKE LOVERS!

DIRECTIONS

In a large bowl, whisk the flour, sugar, baking powder, baking soda, and salt.

In a separate large bowl, whisk the buttermilk, eggs, and vegetable oil until well combined. Pour the buttermilk mixture over the dry ingredients. Stir just until all ingredients are evenly combined. Stir in the mashed banana and coffee.

Heat a cast iron skillet over medium-low heat for 5 minutes, or until very hot. Pour ⅓ cup (78 ml) batter onto the hot skillet and use a spoon, if necessary, to spread the pancake out a bit. Repeat with the remaining batter, but don't overfill the skillet. Cook the pancakes for 1½ to 2 minutes, or until golden brown and bubbles appear on top. With a spatula, flip the pancakes and cook for about 2 more minutes, or until browned on the other side and set in the middle. Repeat with the remaining batter.

JAMAICAN BERRY-COFFEE COMPOTE

YIELD: 4 SERVINGS

The flavors of the Caribbean (think star anise and allspice) pair nicely with mellow coffee to bring out the best in this trio of berries. While it is a delicious breakfast dish, this compote also lends color and flavor to a variety of other dishes. It can be served warm or at room temperature and is great at breakfast on toast or Banana and Coffee–Infused Pancakes (page 42), in desserts such as Coffee Oil–Infused Butter Cake (page 184) or topping your favorite vanilla ice cream, and with a variety of meat dishes.

INGREDIENTS

1 CUP (145 G) FRESH BLACKBERRIES

1 CUP (145 G) FRESH BLUEBERRIES

½ CUP (65 G) FRESH RASPBERRIES

¼ CUP (60 G) FIRMLY PACKED LIGHT BROWN SUGAR

¼ CUP (60 ML) BREWED, COOLED MYSTIC MORNING COFFEE

3 WHOLE ALLSPICE BERRIES, CRACKED (SEE TIP)

1 STAR ANISE

DIRECTIONS

In a medium-size saucepan over medium heat, combine the blackberries, blueberries, raspberries, brown sugar, coffee, allspice, and star anise. Cook the mixture for 5 to 6 minutes, stirring occasionally, or until the sugar is dissolved and the berries are bubbling. Remove the compote from the heat. Remove the allspice and star anise. Cool the compote for about 1 hour; cover and refrigerate for up to 1 month.

TIP: TO CRACK THE ALLSPICE BERRIES, GRIND THEM IN A CLEAN PEPPERMILL, OR PUT THEM IN A NAPKIN AND ROLL OVER THEM WITH A WINE BOTTLE UNTIL CRACKED.

COFFEE-INFUSED
❧ PECAN-CRANBERRY BREAD ❧

YIELD: 1 LOAF, ABOUT 8 SERVINGS

Bake a loaf of this fruity, nutty bread enlivened with a generous splash of brewed coffee, and enjoy it for breakfast with a steaming mug of coffee. You'll love how good your kitchen smells while it's baking and how comforting it is to cut a thick slice for a second helping. It also makes a great mid-morning pick-me-up.

INGREDIENTS

NONSTICK COOKING SPRAY, FOR PREPARING THE PAN

½ CUP (60 G) DRIED CRANBERRIES

¼ CUP (60 ML) ORANGE-FLAVORED LIQUEUR, SUCH AS GRAND MARNIER

1 CUP (235 ML) WATER

2 CUPS (400 G) SUGAR

½ POUND (2 STICKS, OR 225 G) UNSALTED BUTTER, SOFTENED

2 EGGS

2 CUPS (224 G) ALL-PURPOSE FLOUR

2 TEASPOONS BAKING SODA

2 TEASPOONS KOSHER SALT

1 TEASPOON GROUND CINNAMON

¾ CUP (175 ML) BUTTERMILK

½ CUP (55 G) CHOPPED PECANS

½ CUP (120 ML) BREWED, COOLED MYSTIC MORNING COFFEE

2 TABLESPOONS (30 ML) VANILLA EXTRACT

GRATED ZEST OF 1 ORANGE

DIRECTIONS

Preheat the oven to 375°F (190°C, or gas mark 5). Spray a 9-inch (23 cm) loaf pan with cooking spray.

In a medium-size saucepan over high heat, combine the cranberries, liqueur, and water. Bring to a boil, reduce the heat to low, and cook for 4 minutes, stirring occasionally. Let cool.

Meanwhile, in the work bowl of an electric mixer, cream the sugar and butter at high speed until light and fluffy. Add the eggs and beat until light.

In a large bowl, sift together the flour, baking soda, salt, and cinnamon. Add the flour mixture to the creamed mixture alternating with the buttermilk, beating well after each addition. Stir in the cooled cranberry mixture, pecans, coffee, vanilla, and orange zest.

Transfer the batter to the prepared pan. Bake for 55 minutes, or until a tester comes out clean. Cool in the pan for about 10 minutes. Invert the pan onto a cooling rack and cool the loaf thoroughly before slicing.

TIP: THIS LOAF FREEZES VERY WELL, WRAPPED IN FREEZER-QUALITY PLASTIC WRAP, FOR UP TO 3 MONTHS.

CHAPTER

3

TREASURED FAMILY RECIPES

(Smile Jamaica coffee)

Throughout the Caribbean, the cooking is exuberant, lively, and flavorful. And Jamaica, where cooks love using herbs such as thyme, bay, and cilantro, plus lots of fresh garlic, ginger, and hot chillies such as the Scotch bonnet, is certainly no exception. Jamaicans love seasoning their food with jerk seasoning, which contains various spices such as cinnamon and cloves, chillies, and, of course, garlic, and onions. Still, as great as Caribbean food is, there's one ingredient that can make it taste even better—coffee.

Smile Jamaica, a medium-roast coffee with a mellow flavor, is the perfect addition to many of the dishes we remember eating as children. This or another full-bodied coffee heightens the many traditional spices and herbs, imparting delicious flavor to meat, vegetables, and seafood.

In this chapter, you will find a nice sampling of the dishes we grew up loving, from a robust lamb stew flavored with coffee-infused stout, to a classic oxtail casserole seasoned with garlic, simmered in brewed coffee and beef stock, and served with white beans. Enjoy the flavors of authentic Caribbean cooking in your home by preparing the dishes our families still make and love today. Thanks to coffee, all these dishes are better than ever.

❧ MISO AND COFFEE SEA BASS ❧

YIELD: 4 SERVINGS

When cooked, sea bass has a flaky texture and a buttery taste. The sweet notes in the fish perfectly offset the slightly bitter notes in Smile Jamaica coffee.

INGREDIENTS

4 (6- TO 8-OUNCE, OR 170 TO 225 G) SEA BASS FILLETS, CUT 1 INCH (2.5 CM) THICK

½ CUP (125 G) MISO

¼ CUP (60 ML) LOW-SODIUM SOY SAUCE

4 CLOVES GARLIC, MINCED

1 TABLESPOON MINCED FRESH GINGER

2 TEASPOONS FINELY GROUND SMILE JAMAICA COFFEE BEANS

½ CUP UNSALTED BUTTER (1 STICK, OR 113 G) DIVIDED AND SOFTENED

DIRECTIONS

Arrange the sea bass fillets in a large, shallow glass dish. Set aside.

In a medium-size bowl, whisk the miso, soy sauce, garlic, ginger, and coffee until all ingredients are fully incorporated. Pour this marinade over the sea bass and refrigerate for at least 1 hour.

Position an oven rack on the lowest shelf in the oven. Preheat the broiler.

Remove the fillets from the marinade. Arrange them in a single layer on a rimmed, flameproof, nonstick shallow pan. Pour the marinade over the fillets, top each with 2 tablespoons (28 g) butter, and place the pan under the broiler. Broil for about 15 minutes, or until they are cooked through. When done, the fish should be opaque, flake easily, and have a nice golden charred look.

TIP: IF YOU PREFER, SUBSTITUTE GROUPER FOR THE SEA BASS IN THIS DISH.

ROASTED RED SNAPPER MARINATED
❧ WITH ISLAND CITRUS AND HERBS ❧

YIELD: 4 SERVINGS

With its firm-textured flesh and minimal fat content, red snapper benefits from an infusion of flavorful ingredients— not just fresh herbs and chillies, but a generous shake of Marley Coffee Spice Blend. Serve with something simple, like a side of rice and some braised cabbage or callaloo.

INGREDIENTS

4 (8-OUNCE, OR 225 G) RED SNAPPER FILLETS

3 TABLESPOONS (ABOUT 36 G) MARLEY COFFEE SPICE BLEND (PAGE 14)

3 SPRIGS FRESH THYME, CHOPPED

3 CLOVES GARLIC, MINCED

1 SCOTCH BONNET PEPPER, MINCED

KOSHER SALT TO TASTE

JUICE OF 1 LIME

JUICE OF 1 ORANGE

¼ CUP (54.5 G) COCONUT OIL

1 ONION, JULIENNED

1 SWEET PLANTAIN, PEELED AND SLICED

1 LARGE TOMATO, CORED AND DICED

½ CUP (120 ML) DRY WHITE WINE

DIRECTIONS

Preheat a gas grill to 350°F (180°C) or place a grill pan over medium heat.

Arrange the red snapper on a large cutting board. With a sharp knife, make two 1-inch (2.5 cm) slits on both sides of each fillet.

In a blender or food processor, combine the Marley Coffee Spice Blend, thyme, garlic, Scotch bonnet pepper, salt, lime juice, and orange juice until just blended. Season both sides of the snapper with this mixture and rub some into the slits. Brush both sides with coconut oil.

Arrange the snapper fillets on heavy-duty aluminum foil, making sure the foil overhangs about 1 inch (2.5 cm) on each end. Top with the onion, plantain, and tomato. Drizzle a little white wine over each fillet. Place another piece of foil on top of the fish and seal the edges tightly.

Grill the red snapper for about 25 minutes, or until it flakes easily with a fork. Remove from the grill and let rest for 2 to 3 minutes. Carefully open the foil package. Transfer the fish and vegetables to a serving dish.

NOTE: This dish is traditionally made with a whole red snapper, which can be hard to find. If you can't find it, it is just as good made with fillets. And if red snapper is unavailable, substitute another white fish.

❖ BROWN STEW CHICKEN ❖

YIELD: 6 SERVINGS

Brewed coffee and a generous shake of Marley Coffee Spice Blend (page 14) combine to give this old-fashioned, very traditional chicken stew a real boost of flavor. It's a one-pot dinner that makes use of Caribbean seasonings and that's easy to pull off, even for beginners. Make it ahead and reheat when you're ready to eat.

INGREDIENTS

2 (3-POUND, OR 1.36 KG) CHICKENS, QUARTERED

1 TABLESPOON MARLEY COFFEE SPICE BLEND (PAGE 14)

1 CUP (112 G) ALL-PURPOSE FLOUR

KOSHER SALT AND FRESHLY GROUND BLACK PEPPER TO TASTE

1 CUP (218 G) COCONUT OIL

1 RED BELL PEPPER, CORED, SEEDED, AND DICED

½ YELLOW ONION, DICED

3 CLOVES GARLIC, MINCED

2 TABLESPOONS CHOPPED FRESH THYME LEAVES

3 SCALLIONS (WHITE AND LIGHT GREEN PARTS), SLICED THIN, DIVIDED

2 STALKS CELERY, DICED

2 BIRD PEPPERS

1 CUP (235 ML) CHICKEN STOCK OR BROTH

½ CUP (120 ML) BREWED, COOLED SMILE JAMAICA COFFEE

3 TABLESPOONS (48 G) TOMATO PASTE

3 TABLESPOONS (45 ML) BROWNING AND SEASONING SAUCE, SUCH AS GRAVY MASTER OR GRACE BRAND

FRESH PARSLEY, FOR GARNISH

DIRECTIONS

In a large bowl, toss the chicken parts with the Marley Coffee Spice Blend. On a large plate, season the flour with salt and pepper, and whisk to combine. Coat the chicken pieces with the flour mixture, turning to make sure they are evenly covered.

In a large, heavy pan over medium heat, heat the coconut oil until very hot. Carefully add the chicken pieces, skin-side down. Sauté for 6 minutes per side, or until golden brown. Remove the chicken from the pan and set aside.

To the pan, add the red bell pepper, onion, garlic, thyme, half of the scallions, celery, and bird peppers. Sauté for about 3 minutes, or until the onion begins to brown.

Stir in the chicken stock, coffee, tomato paste, and browning and seasoning sauce. Cook for 2 minutes, stirring. Return the chicken to the pan, cover, and simmer for 45 minutes, or until the chicken is thoroughly cooked. Taste, and add more salt and pepper, as desired. Garnish with the remaining scallions and parsley.

TIP: SERVE THIS HOMEY STEW WITH WHITE RICE OR WITH RICE AND PEAS.

COFFEE STOUT LAMB STEW INFUSED
❧ WITH COFFEE BEANS ❧

YIELD: 6 SERVINGS

Coffee Stout (page 129) ensures that the vegetables in this stew are especially flavorful and the lamb is fork-tender. The variety of vegetables lends color and a slightly crunchy texture. It's really the marriage of red wine, coffee stout, and finely ground Smile Jamaica coffee beans that sets this swoon-worthy stew apart.

INGREDIENTS

3 POUNDS (1.36 KG) LAMB STEW MEAT, CUT INTO 1-INCH (2.5 CM) CHUNKS

1 BAY LEAF

1¼ CUPS (285 ML) EXTRA-VIRGIN OLIVE OIL, DIVIDED

3 CLOVES GARLIC, CHOPPED

1 QUART (946 ML) BEEF STOCK OR BROTH

1 CUP (235 ML) DRY RED WINE

¼ CUP (65 G) TOMATO PASTE

2 CELERY STALKS, CHOPPED

1 LARGE YELLOW ONION, CHOPPED

2 SPRIGS FRESH THYME, CHOPPED

3 TABLESPOONS (ABOUT 36 G) MARLEY COFFEE SPICE BLEND (PAGE 14)

1 TABLESPOON FINELY GROUND SMILE JAMAICA COFFEE BEANS

1 CUP (112 G) ALL-PURPOSE FLOUR

1 POUND (454 G) BABY CARROTS

2 PARSNIPS, PEELED AND CHOPPED INTO ½-INCH (1 CM) CUBES

1 YAM, PEELED AND CHOPPED INTO ½-INCH (1 CM) CUBES

1 RUTABAGA, PEELED AND CHOPPED INTO ½-INCH (1 CM) CUBES

1 RED OR GREEN BELL PEPPER, CORED, SEEDED, AND CHOPPED

1 PLANTAIN, PEELED AND CHOPPED

¼ HEAD GREEN CABBAGE, TOUGH LEAVES REMOVED, SLICED

1 BUNCH FRESH CILANTRO, STEMMED AND CHOPPED

1 CUP (235 ML) COFFEE STOUT (PAGE 129)

KOSHER SALT AND FRESHLY GROUND BLACK PEPPER TO TASTE

DIRECTIONS

In a 10-quart stockpot over high heat, combine the lamb and bay leaf with enough water to cover. Bring to a boil. Reduce the heat to low, and simmer, covered, for about 45 minutes. Carefully pour off the water. Add ¼ cup (60 ml) olive oil and the garlic. Sauté for 2 or 3 minutes, or until the garlic softens.

Stir in the beef stock, red wine, tomato paste, celery, onion, thyme, Marley Coffee Spice Blend, and coffee beans. Bring to a boil. Reduce the heat to low. Simmer, covered, for about 45 minutes, stirring occasionally.

While the stew simmers, make a roux. In a small, heavy saucepan, whisk the remaining olive oil with the flour. Turn the heat to medium and cook the mixture, stirring, until it is smooth and light brown. Measure ¼ cup (60 g) roux and refrigerate the rest.

To the stew, stir in the rest of the vegetables, the cilantro, coffee stout, and ¼ cup (60 g) roux. Season with salt and pepper. Simmer, covered, for about 1 hour, or until the vegetables and lamb are tender.

NOTE: Wondering what roux is? Essentially, it's a mixture of flour and fat slowly cooked and used to thicken soups, stews, and sauces. The source of the fat could be butter or oil, or it could just as easily be pan drippings.

❧ CARIBBEAN COFFEE-BRAISED OXTAILS ❧

YIELD: 4 SERVINGS

Chef Max's mother makes her version of this classic dish quite often. The twist? Adding some Smile Jamaica coffee, our signature blend that contains Blue Mountain coffee. Thanks to its balanced acidity and rich flavor, this hearty stew quickly became a favorite for both of us. It's a real crowd (and mother) pleaser. This is delicious served with coconut peas and rice.

INGREDIENTS

3 POUNDS (1.36 KG) OXTAILS

¼ CUP (65 G) TOMATO PASTE

3 CLOVES GARLIC, MINCED

1 BUNCH FRESH THYME, STEMMED AND CHOPPED

3 TABLESPOONS (ABOUT 36 G) MARLEY COFFEE SPICE BLEND (PAGE 14)

2 TEASPOONS (10 ML) BROWNING AND SEASONING SAUCE, SUCH AS GRAVY MASTER OR GRACE BRAND

KOSHER SALT AND FRESHLY GROUND BLACK PEPPER TO TASTE

¼ CUP (55 G) COCONUT OIL

2 LARGE CARROTS, CHOPPED

2 CELERY STALKS, CHOPPED

1 YELLOW OR WHITE ONION, CHOPPED

1 RED BELL PEPPER, CORED, SEEDED, AND DICED

2 BAY LEAVES

¼ CUP (28 G) ALL-PURPOSE FLOUR

3 CUPS (705 ML) BEEF STOCK OR BROTH

1 CUP (235 ML) BREWED SMILE JAMAICA COFFEE

1 SCOTCH BONNET PEPPER, CHOPPED

1 (15.5-OUNCE, OR 439 G) CAN WHITE BEANS, RINSED AND DRAINED

DIRECTIONS

Place the oxtails in a large bowl. In a medium-size bowl, thoroughly mix the tomato paste, garlic, thyme, Marley Coffee Spice Blend, browning and seasoning sauce, salt, and pepper. Add this to the oxtails and stir them to coat with the seasoning mix.

In a large, deep pot over medium heat, heat the coconut oil until very hot. Remove the oxtails from the seasoning mix and transfer them to the pot. Sear for about 4 minutes per side, or until golden brown. Don't crowd the pan—you may need to do this in several batches so they don't steam. Transfer the oxtails to the large bowl and set aside.

Return the pot to medium heat. Sauté the carrots, celery, onion, red bell pepper, bay leaves, and flour for about 3 minutes, or until the vegetables begin to color. Stir in the beef stock, coffee, and Scotch bonnet pepper. Bring to a boil. Add the oxtails, with their juices, to the pot. Reduce the heat to low, cover the pot, and simmer for about 2½ hours, or until the oxtails are tender.

Uncover the pot, increase the heat to medium, and add the beans. Stirring occasionally, let the mixture cook for about 6 minutes, or until the liquid thickens to a sauce-like consistency. This is delicious served with coconut peas and rice.

NOTE: Coconut oil has great flavor as well as a higher smoke point than many other oils, which makes it ideal for sautéing.

ISLAND SALMON BURGERS WITH AVOCADO–BLACK BEAN SALSA ❧ AND LEMON ZEST MAYO ❧

YIELD: 4 SERVINGS

A generous dollop of Marley Coffee Spice Blend (page 14) takes these beautiful burgers out of the realm of ordinary. Cutting the richness of the salmon while simultaneously imbuing it with a dark, smoky flavor, this spice blend pays big flavor dividends. Try these burgers on whole-wheat buns, glossed with homemade lemony mayo, and flanked by an avocado–black bean salsa. This salsa goes with a lot—think tacos of all kinds or as a topping for fish. Let Island Time begin.

INGREDIENTS

FOR AVOCADO-BLACK BEAN SALSA:

1 (15.5-OUNCE, OR 439 G) CAN BLACK BEANS, RINSED AND DRAINED

1 AVOCADO, PEELED, PITTED, AND DICED

1 MANGO, PEELED, PITTED, AND DICED

¼ CUP (40 G) DICED RED ONION

½ BUNCH FRESH CILANTRO, STEMMED AND CHOPPED

¼ CUP (60 ML) EXTRA-VIRGIN OLIVE OIL

JUICE OF ½ LIME

1 CLOVE GARLIC, MINCED

FOR LEMON ZEST MAYO:

½ CUP (115 G) MAYONNAISE

JUICE OF ½ LEMON

ZEST OF 1 LEMON

1 CLOVE GARLIC, MINCED

1 TABLESPOON CHOPPED FRESH CILANTRO LEAVES

FOR SALMON BURGERS:

2 CUPS (ABOUT 450 G) DICED BONELESS SKINLESS SALMON FILLET

2 EGGS, LIGHTLY BEATEN

2 SCALLIONS (WHITE AND LIGHT GREEN PARTS), CHOPPED

¼ CUP (40 G) DICED YELLOW ONION

¼ CUP (38 G) DICED TRICOLOR PEPPER (A MIX OF RED, GREEN, AND YELLOW PEPPERS), CORED, SEEDED, AND DICED

¼ CUP (40 G) DICED FRESH PINEAPPLE

2 TABLESPOONS (30 G) DIJON MUSTARD, SUCH AS GREY POUPON

1 TABLESPOON CHOPPED FRESH CILANTRO LEAVES

1 GARLIC CLOVE, MINCED

1 TABLESPOON MARLEY COFFEE SPICE BLEND (PAGE 14)

½ CUP (57.5 G) DRY BREAD CRUMBS

1 TABLESPOON (30 ML) EXTRA-VIRGIN OLIVE OIL

SOFTENED UNSALTED BUTTER, FOR THE BUNS

4 WHOLE-WHEAT HAMBURGER BUNS

MICROGREENS, FOR GARNISH (OPTIONAL)

DIRECTIONS

TO MAKE THE AVOCADO-BLACK BEAN SALSA:

In a medium-size bowl, stir together all of the salsa ingredients. Cover and refrigerate.

TO MAKE THE LEMON ZEST MAYO:

In another medium-size bowl, whisk the mayonnaise, lemon juice, lemon zest, garlic, and cilantro. Cover and refrigerate.

TO MAKE THE SALMON BURGERS:

In a large bowl, combine the salmon, eggs, scallions, onion, pepper, pineapple, mustard, cilantro, garlic, Marley Coffee Spice Blend, bread crumbs, and olive oil. Form the mixture into 4 patties.

Preheat the broiler to medium. Place the burgers under the broiler for 10 minutes, turning once, or until thoroughly cooked. Spread butter on the cut sides of the buns and toast under the broiler for 30 seconds, or until golden and crisp. Arrange a burger on the bottom half of each bun. Top with salsa, lemon zest mayo, and the other half of the bun. Garnish with microgreens, if desired.

TIP: IF YOU LIKE, SERVE THESE BURGERS OPEN-FACED BY OMITTING THE TOP HALF OF THE BUN.

❧ CURRY AND COFFEE-BRAISED LAMB ❧

YIELD: 4 SERVINGS

For this traditional Sunday dinner dish, Chef Max's mother would always use goat. In this updated version, lamb, which is less gamey, gets a double boost of flavor from Smile Jamaica coffee and Marley Coffee Spice Blend (page 14). Making this wonderful dish ahead of time is advisable so the flavors have time to meld and deepen.

INGREDIENTS

2 TABLESPOONS (30 ML) EXTRA-VIRGIN OLIVE OIL

¼ CUP (25 G) CURRY POWDER

¼ CUP (65 G) TOMATO PASTE

3 TABLESPOONS (ABOUT 36 G) MARLEY COFFEE SPICE BLEND (PAGE 14)

3 CLOVES GARLIC, MINCED

2 SPRIGS FRESH THYME

2 BAY LEAVES, CRUMBLED

1 (4-POUND, OR 1.8 KG) BONE-IN LEG OF LAMB

KOSHER SALT AND FRESHLY GROUND BLACK PEPPER TO TASTE

1 LARGE CARROT, CHOPPED

1 MEDIUM-SIZE WHITE OR YELLOW ONION, CHOPPED

¼ STALK CELERY, CHOPPED

2 CUPS (475 ML) VEGETABLE STOCK OR BROTH

1 CUP (235 ML) BREWED, COOLED SMILE JAMAICA COFFEE

DIRECTIONS

Preheat the oven to 400°F (200°C, or gas mark 6).

In a medium-size bowl, thoroughly mix the olive oil, curry powder, tomato paste, Marley Coffee Spice Blend, garlic, thyme, and bay leaves. Rub the lamb all over with this mixture. Season with salt and pepper.

In a large roasting pan, combine the carrot, onion, and celery. Pour the vegetable stock and the coffee over the vegetables. Stir to combine. Arrange the lamb on top of the vegetables. Cover the roasting pan with aluminum foil. Bake for 2½ hours, or until the lamb is fork-tender. Let rest for 10 to 15 minutes before slicing.

TIP: FEEL FREE TO ADD OTHER VEGETABLES TO THIS DISH, AND TO SUBSTITUTE CHICKEN STOCK FOR THE VEGETABLE STOCK.

I THINK OF MYSELF AS A SERIAL ENTREPRENEUR. I DON'T SEE THINGS THAT I CAN'T DO. A "RASTA-PRENEUR," THAT'S WHAT THEY CALL ME! FOR ME, THE PRINCIPLES OF THE LION ARE IMPORTANT. THAT'S MY STAMP. THE LION STANDS FOR STRENGTH AND COURAGE. THE LION KNOWS WHAT HE IS MEANT TO BE, NOT WHAT HE SHOULD BE, OR WHAT YOU THINK HE SHOULD BE. THE LION DOESN'T CHANGE. LIONS DON'T DO THINGS GOOD OR BAD. THEY JUST DO. NO ONE TELLS THE LION, "GOOD LION," OR "BAD LION." THE LION JUST IS. WHAT HE DOES IS WHAT HE DOES.

COFFEE-INFUSED PEPPER SHRIMP

YIELD: 4 SERVINGS

This traditional dish is eaten often in Jamaica, where it's common to leave on both the heads and the shells of the tiger shrimp. For maximum flavor, we like to remove the shells but leave the heads on. In this high-flavor dish, the shrimp are infused with coconut milk as well as Smile Jamaica coffee.

INGREDIENTS

2 TABLESPOONS (28 G) COCONUT OIL (SEE NOTE)

¼ CUP (40 G) DICED YELLOW OR WHITE ONION (ABOUT ¼ ONION)

2 CLOVES GARLIC, MINCED

1 SPRIG FRESH THYME

1½ POUNDS (680 G) TIGER SHRIMP, HEADS LEFT ON, CLEANED, SHELLS REMOVED

2 TOMATILLOS, DICED

3 TABLESPOONS (19 G) CURRY POWDER

1 CUP (240 ML) COCONUT MILK

3 TABLESPOONS (45 ML) BREWED SMILE JAMAICA COFFEE

1 TABLESPOON (15 ML) HOT SAUCE

¼ POUND (1 STICK, OR 113 G) UNSALTED BUTTER

TOASTED COCONUT FLAKES, FOR GARNISH

FRESH CILANTRO, CHOPPED, FOR GARNISH

DIRECTIONS

In a large wok or sauté pan over medium-high heat, heat the coconut oil until very hot. Add the onion, garlic, and thyme. Sauté for 2 minutes, or until the onion starts to color.

Add the shrimp, tomatillos, and the curry powder. Cook for 1 minute, stirring. Stir in the coconut milk, coffee, pepper sauce, and butter. Reduce the heat to low and simmer the mixture for 2 minutes, or until the shrimp are cooked through. Remove the shrimp to a platter and keep warm.

Continue to cook the sauce for another 2 minutes, or until reduced by half. Ladle the sauce over the shrimp. Garnish with toasted coconut flakes and cilantro.

NOTE: Tiger shrimp can be hard to find in some markets, but you may easily substitute jumbo shrimp in this recipe. And when it comes to coconut milk, coconut oil, and coconut vinegar, we prefer Grace Foods brand.

COFFEE JERK SALMON

YIELD: 4 TO 6 SERVINGS

Salmon's inherently rich flavor is heightened here by a delicious marinade featuring garlic, orange juice, and homemade jerk seasoning. If you don't have time to make your own jerk seasoning, Grace Foods makes an excellent one. When you make this dish, allow plenty of time for the salmon to marinate for best results.

INGREDIENTS

1 TABLESPOON JERK SEASONING (PAGE 17)

3 TABLESPOONS (42 G) COCONUT OIL

2 CLOVES GARLIC, PEELED AND MINCED

¼ CUP (60 ML) BREWED, COOLED SMILE JAMAICA COFFEE

½ BUNCH FRESH CILANTRO, STEMMED AND CHOPPED

JUICE OF ¼ ORANGE

2 POUNDS (908 G) FRESH ATLANTIC SALMON FILLETS OR STEAKS

DIRECTIONS

In a large, shallow bowl, stir together the jerk seasoning, coconut oil, garlic, coffee, cilantro, and orange juice. Place the salmon in this mixture and marinate in the refrigerator for 20 to 30 minutes, or overnight.

Preheat the oven to 350°F (180°C, or gas mark 4). Preheat a large grill pan over medium heat. Remove the salmon from the marinade, discard the marinade, and grill the salmon in the hot grill pan for about 3 minutes per side. Transfer the salmon to a large baking dish. Bake for about 4 minutes, or until done. The salmon will be opaque and pink, and the interior will be 155°F (68°C) measured with an instant-read thermometer. Serve with couscous, if desired.

TIP: FOR COLOR AND FLAVOR, SERVE THE COOKED SALMON WITH AN AVOCADO SALSA.

PANFRIED GROUPER
❖ WITH COFFEE-SPICED FRUIT CHUTNEY ❖

YIELD: 4 TO 6 SERVINGS

Max's mother is a big fan of grouper, which, along with red snapper, is a popular fish to eat in the Bahamas. This dish gets spiced up a little thanks to the addition of a coffee- and cinnamon-flavored chutney.

INGREDIENTS

FOR SPICED FRUIT CHUTNEY:

¼ CUP (60 ML) BREWED, COOLED SMILE JAMAICA COFFEE

1 BAY LEAF

1 SHALLOT, MINCED

2 PEARS (YOUR FAVORITE VARIETY), CORED, PEELED, AND DICED

¼ PINEAPPLE, DICED

¼ CUP (60 G) PACKED LIGHT BROWN SUGAR

1 TEASPOON FRESHLY GRATED LEMON ZEST

2 TABLESPOONS (30 ML) FRESHLY SQUEEZED LEMON JUICE

1 TEASPOON FINELY CHOPPED FRESH GINGER

PINCH GROUND CINNAMON

2 TABLESPOONS (30 ML) CHAMPAGNE VINEGAR OR
  APPLE CIDER VINEGAR

FOR GROUPER:

2 POUNDS (908 G) GROUPER FILLETS

KOSHER SALT AND FRESHLY GROUND BLACK PEPPER TO TASTE

1 TABLESPOON MARLEY COFFEE SPICE BLEND (PAGE 14), DIVIDED

2 CUPS (224 G) ALL-PURPOSE FLOUR

½ CUP (109 G) COCONUT OIL

LIME WEDGES, FOR GARNISH

DIRECTIONS

TO MAKE THE SPICED FRUIT CHUTNEY:

In a medium-size saucepan over medium heat, combine the coffee, bay leaf, and shallot. Bring to a simmer. Add the pears, pineapple, brown sugar, lemon zest, lemon juice, ginger, cinnamon, and vinegar. Reduce the heat to low and simmer for 25 to 30 minutes, or until the liquid is reduced by half and the fruit is fork-tender. Cover the chutney and set aside.

TO MAKE THE GROUPER:

Preheat the oven to 350°F (180°C, or gas mark 4). Place the grouper in a shallow pan. Season it with salt, pepper, and 1½ teaspoons Marley Coffee Spice Blend.

In a medium-size bowl, combine the flour with the remaining 1½ teaspoons Marley Coffee Spice Blend. Coat the fish with the seasoned flour, shaking off any excess. Discard any remaining flour.

In a large skillet or sauté pan over medium heat, heat the coconut oil until very hot. Place the fish in the pan and sauté for about 3 minutes per side, flipping once with a spatula. When the fish is golden brown on both sides, transfer it to a baking dish and bake for about 5 minutes, or until thoroughly cooked. The fish is done when it flakes easily. Garnish the fish with lime wedges and serve with the chutney.

TIP: SUBSTITUTE ANY WHITE FISH FOR THE GROUPER.

BROILED MAHIMAHI WITH CALLALOO
❧ AND COFFEE BUTTER ❧

YIELD: 4 SERVINGS

Smile Jamaica coffee and a hit of Marley Coffee Spice Blend (page 14) raise the flavor profile of this Jamaican favorite considerably, so make plenty and expect your friends to request seconds.

INGREDIENTS

FOR CALLALOO:

2 BUNCHES CALLALOO, LEAVES AND SOFT STEMS ONLY

¼ CUP (55 G) COCONUT OIL

1 MEDIUM-SIZE YELLOW ONION, DICED

1 MEDIUM-SIZE TOMATO, CORED AND DICED

2 CLOVES GARLIC, PEELED AND MINCED

1 SPRIG FRESH THYME, STEMMED AND CHOPPED

½ SCOTCH BONNET PEPPER, DICED

¼ CUP (60 ML) BREWED SMILE JAMAICA COFFEE

2 TABLESPOONS (¼ STICK, OR 28 G) UNSALTED BUTTER, SOFTENED

FOR MAHIMAHI:

1½ POUNDS (680 G) MAHIMAHI FILLETS

1 TABLESPOON MARLEY COFFEE SPICE BLEND (PAGE 14)

KOSHER SALT AND FRESHLY GROUND BLACK PEPPER TO TASTE

¼ POUND (1 STICK, OR 113 G) UNSALTED BUTTER, SOFTENED

GRILLED LEMONS (PAGE 149), FOR GARNISH, OPTIONAL

DIRECTIONS

TO MAKE THE CALLALOO:

Soak the callaloo leaves and soft stems in a large bowl of ice-cold water for 10 minutes. Scoop the leaves and stems out of the water. Rinse them under cold running water, place in a colander, and drain very well.

In a large skillet or sauté pan over medium heat, heat the coconut oil for 1 minute, or until very hot. Add the onion, tomato, garlic, thyme, and Scotch bonnet pepper. Sauté for about 3 minutes, or until the garlic begins to color. Add the callaloo and coffee. Cook for about 2 minutes more, stirring constantly. Remove from the heat, fold in the butter, and set aside.

TO MAKE THE MAHIMAHI:

Preheat the broiler. Place the mahimahi on a rimmed baking sheet. Sprinkle with the Marley Coffee Spice Blend, salt, and pepper. Rub the mahimahi with the butter. Place the baking sheet on a lower oven rack 4 to 6 inches (10 to 15 cm) from the heat. Broil for about 8 minutes. Move it to the top rack and broil for 2 minutes more, or until cooked throughout and nicely browned on top. Serve with the callaloo and some grilled lemons, if desired.

TIP: CAN'T FIND CALLALOO? SUBSTITUTE COLLARD GREENS.

COD FRITTERS WITH COFFEE-INFUSED
❧ CREOLE REMOULADE ❧

YIELD: 4 TO 6 SERVINGS

Classic remoulade is a creamy, mayo-based herb sauce sometimes containing capers or chopped gherkins. It's the perfect dipping sauce for the flavorful, crisp cod fritters beloved in the Caribbean. As an appetizer, pair them with a frosty glass of Coffee Stout (page 129).

INGREDIENTS

FOR REMOULADE:

2 CUPS (450 G) MAYONNAISE

3 TABLESPOONS (45 ML) HOT SAUCE OR TO TASTE

JUICE OF 1 LIME

2 TABLESPOONS CHOPPED FRESH CILANTRO LEAVES

2 TABLESPOONS (17 G) BLACKENED SEASONING

2 CLOVES GARLIC, MINCED

FOR FRITTERS:

2 POUNDS (908 G) SALTED COD

1 TABLESPOON COCONUT OIL

4 SCALLIONS (WHITE AND LIGHT GREEN PARTS), SLICED

1 RED BELL PEPPER, CORED, SEEDED, AND MINCED

¼ MEDIUM-SIZE YELLOW ONION, DICED

2 CLOVES GARLIC, MINCED

½ BUNCH FRESH CILANTRO, STEMMED AND CHOPPED

1 TABLESPOON MARLEY COFFEE SPICE BLEND

1 TABLESPOON CHOPPED FRESH THYME LEAVES

3 CUPS (336 G) ALL-PURPOSE FLOUR

1 TABLESPOON BAKING POWDER

3 EGGS, LIGHTLY BEATEN

2½ CUPS (595 ML) ICE-COLD WATER

VEGETABLE OIL, FOR FRYING

FRESH PARSLEY, CHOPPED, FOR GARNISH

DIRECTIONS

TO MAKE THE REMOULADE:

In a medium-size bowl, stir together the remoulade ingredients until mixed. Cover and refrigerate until needed.

TO MAKE THE FRITTERS:

In a large bowl, combine the cod with enough cold water to cover and set aside for 1 hour. Drain the cod and return it to the bowl. Cover it with more cold water. After another hour, drain and repeat.

In a medium-size saucepan of boiling water over high heat, cook the salted cod for 8 to 10 minutes, or until it flakes easily when pricked with a fork. Drain and transfer to a baking sheet to cool for a few minutes. Flake when cool enough to handle.

Heat a large skillet or sauté pan over medium heat for 1 minute, or until very hot. Add the coconut oil, scallions, red bell pepper, onion, garlic, cilantro, Marley Coffee Spice Blend, and thyme. Sauté for 2 minutes, or until the vegetables start to color. Remove from the heat and set aside to cool.

In a large bowl, stir together the flour and baking powder. Add the eggs and ice-cold water. Whisk until very smooth. Stir in the flaked cod and vegetable mixture, stirring until all ingredients are well incorporated. Form balls of batter and place them on a plate. Refrigerate the fritters for about 30 minutes.

In an electric fryer set to medium or a cast iron skillet over medium heat, add vegetable oil to a depth of about 3 inches (7.5 cm). Drop a few fritters into the hot oil. Don't crowd the pan. Fry the fritters for 3 minutes, or until cooked throughout and golden brown. Transfer to paper towels to drain. Repeat with the remaining batter. Garnish with parsley and serve with the remoulade.

TIP: ALLOW PLENTY OF TIME FOR SOAKING THE COD IN THE COLD WATER 3 TIMES, A PROCESS THAT GETS RID OF SOME OF THE SALT IN THE FISH AND IS ESSENTIAL IF YOU WANT YOUR FRITTERS TO BE FLAVORFUL.

CARIBBEAN PAN-SEARED SNAPPER ESCOVITCH

YIELD: 4 SERVINGS

You can partially prepare this spicy, colorful dish a day in advance by cooking the vegetables ahead of time. Reheat the vegetable mixture while you sauté the fish. Serve this with Coffee Stout (page 129) for an amazing meal.

INGREDIENTS

6 TABLESPOONS (90 ML) EXTRA-VIRGIN OLIVE OIL, DIVIDED

1 SMALL YELLOW ONION, CORED, SEEDED, AND JULIENNED

½ YELLOW BELL PEPPER, CORED, SEEDED, AND JULIENNED

½ RED BELL PEPPER, CORED, SEEDED, AND JULIENNED

½ GREEN BELL PEPPER, CORED, SEEDED, AND JULIENNED

2 CARROTS, JULIENNED

2 SCALLIONS (WHITE AND LIGHT GREEN PARTS), SLICED

3 CLOVES GARLIC, MINCED

KOSHER SALT AND FRESHLY GROUND BLACK PEPPER TO TASTE

3 TABLESPOONS (45 ML) WHITE VINEGAR

JUICE OF ½ LIME

JUICE OF ½ ORANGE

3 TABLESPOONS CHOPPED FRESH CILANTRO LEAVES

2 WHOLE SMILE JAMAICA COFFEE BEANS

1 TEASPOON SUGAR

1½ POUNDS (680 G) RED SNAPPER FILLETS OR WHOLE SNAPPER

2 TABLESPOONS (ABOUT 24 G) MARLEY COFFEE SPICE BLEND (PAGE 14)

1 SCOTCH BONNET PEPPER, FINELY DICED

1 LEMON, CUT INTO WEDGES

DIRECTIONS

Preheat the oven to 375°F (190°C, or gas mark 5).

In a large ovenproof skillet or sauté pan over medium-high heat, heat 2 tablespoons (30 ml) olive oil until very hot. Add the onion, yellow, red, and green bell peppers, carrots, scallions, and garlic. Season with salt and pepper. Sauté the vegetables for 3 minutes, or until they soften and begin to wilt.

Stir in the vinegar, lime juice, orange juice, cilantro, coffee beans, and sugar. Bring the mixture to a simmer over medium heat. Reduce the heat to low and cook for 2 minutes, stirring, or until the liquid is hot and bubbly.

Season the snapper fillets with salt and pepper. Sprinkle on the Marley Coffee Spice Blend and Scotch bonnet pepper. In another large ovenproof skillet or sauté pan over high heat, heat the remaining 4 tablespoons (60 ml) olive oil until it smokes. Sear the fillets, skin-side down, for 3 minutes. With a large spatula, flip the fillets and cook them on the other side for about 3 minutes, or until the flesh is firm and flaky and the skin is bright orange. Place the skillet in the oven for 15 to 20 minutes, or until the fillets are cooked through.

Remove the coffee beans from the vegetable mixture and discard. Spoon the vegetable mixture over the fillets. Garnish with the lemon wedges.

TIP: YOU CAN CHOP THE GARLIC VERY FINELY BY HAND, OR PUT IT THROUGH A GARLIC PRESS. WHICHEVER METHOD YOU CHOOSE, USE ONLY VERY FRESH GARLIC AS ITS FLAVOR IS IMPORTANT IN THIS DISH.

4

VEGETARIAN FARE—PURE AND SIMPLE

(One Love coffee)

One Love, a single-origin 100 percent Yirgacheffe coffee from Ethiopia, the birthplace of coffee, possesses hints of spices and vanilla, along with floral and berry notes that perfectly complement vegetables of every kind. Simmer root vegetables in a coffee-infused stock to make an exotic coconut curry root vegetable stew, sprinkle finely ground coffee beans into a rub to use on vegetables to coax out every last bit of sweetness as they roast, or prep a sauce for a stir-fry that combines brewed coffee with chili paste, brown sugar, and soy sauce.

Coffee lends a mellow flavor to a variety of meat-free dishes, from simple side dishes to more complicated main courses. You'll love our Herb- and Garlic-Roasted Eggplant (page 82) topped with marinara sauce and mozzarella cheese and our Green Beans and Honey-Roasted Almonds (page 74) spiced with Marley Coffee Spice Blend.

Think of these recipes as a guide, and incorporate or substitute your favorite vegetables as inspired. And don't skip this chapter if you're into eating meat. Nearly everything here can be served as a side next to your favorite meat, chicken, or seafood dish. Or whip up a couple and serve them together at the same meal. These are colorful, satisfying, and at their flavorful best thanks to coffee.

GREEN BEANS AND
❧ HONEY-ROASTED ALMONDS ❧

YIELD: 4 SERVINGS

Here, Marley Coffee Spice Blend (page 14) enhances crisp green beans, which take on a delicious sweet-savory flavor when cooked with honey-roasted almonds. These make a great side for Grilled Honey-Glazed Chicken (page 108) or Miso and Coffee Sea Bass (page 50).

INGREDIENTS

2 TABLESPOONS (16 G) SESAME SEEDS

2 TABLESPOONS (ABOUT 24 G) MARLEY COFFEE SPICE BLEND (PAGE 14)

1 POUND (454 G) GREEN BEANS, TRIMMED AND CLEANED

3 TABLESPOONS (45 ML) EXTRA-VIRGIN OLIVE OIL

2 CLOVES GARLIC, MINCED

¼ CUP (28 G) FINELY CHOPPED HONEY-ROASTED ALMONDS

¼ CUP (60 ML) CHICKEN STOCK OR BROTH

KOSHER SALT AND FRESHLY GROUND BLACK PEPPER TO TASTE

DIRECTIONS

In a small bowl, stir together the sesame seeds and Marley Coffee Spice Blend. Set aside.

Bring a large saucepan of water to a boil over medium-high heat. Add the green beans, cover, and cook for 10 to 15 minutes, or until crisp-tender and still bright green. Drain and set aside.

In a large skillet over low heat, heat the olive oil until very hot. Add the garlic and almonds. Cook for 30 seconds, stirring. Stir in the chicken stock and season with salt and pepper. Add the green beans and cook for 3 minutes, or until very hot and coated with the stock mixture.

Transfer the beans to a serving dish and sprinkle with the spiced sesame seeds. Serve hot.

TIP: TO MAKE A VEGETARIAN VERSION OF THIS DISH, USE VEGETABLE STOCK OR BROTH IN PLACE OF CHICKEN STOCK.

VEGETABLES STIR-FRIED
❧ IN COFFEE-INFUSED OIL ❧

YIELD: 4 SERVINGS

This dish showcases vegetables in their pure and simple state—what could be better? The Coffee and Star Anise–Infused Oil (page 24) pairs especially well with assertively flavored vegetables like bok choy, peppers, and onions. Serve this with Coffee Jerk Salmon (page 64) or Coffee Stout Lamb Stew Infused with Coffee Beans (page 54) for a refreshing meal.

INGREDIENTS

2 TEASPOONS (10 ML) SESAME OIL

2 CARROTS, JULIENNED

1 HEAD BOK CHOY, WASHED AND TRIMMED

1 STALK CELERY, SLICED INTO THIN STRIPS

½ CUP (80 G) SLICED YELLOW ONION (ABOUT 1 SMALL ONION)

1 (4-OUNCE, OR 115 G) CAN BAMBOO SHOOTS, DRAINED

½ HEAD BROCCOLI, CUT INTO FLORETS

¼ CUP (38 G) RED BELL PEPPER STRIPS

¼ CUP (38 G) GREEN BELL PEPPER STRIPS

1 (15-OUNCE, OR 425 G) CAN BABY CORN, DRAINED

½ CUP (40 G) SHIITAKE MUSHROOMS, SLICED

2 CLOVES GARLIC, MINCED

½ CUP (120 ML) TERIYAKI SAUCE

¼ CUP (60 ML) COFFEE AND STAR ANISE-INFUSED OIL (PAGE 24)

2 TABLESPOONS (16 G) SESAME SEEDS

DIRECTIONS

In a medium-size or large wok over medium heat, heat the sesame oil until very hot. Add the carrots, bok choy, celery, onion, bamboo shoots, broccoli, red and green bell peppers, baby corn, and mushrooms. Stir-fry for 5 minutes, or until the vegetables are crisp but soft. Stir in the garlic, teriyaki sauce, and infused oil. Simmer for 2 minutes. Transfer to a serving bowl. Sprinkle with the sesame seeds and serve.

TIP: SERVE THIS OVER RICE OR YOUR FAVORITE NOODLES.

COFFEE SPICE–ROASTED
❧ BRUSSELS SPROUTS ❧

YIELD: 4 SERVINGS

Even if you're not a Brussels sprouts fan, you will be after a taste of these deliciously caramelized, garlicky sprouts. If you like your veggies spicy, increase the amount of Marley Coffee Spice Blend (page 14). These go nicely with Caribbean Pan-Seared Snapper Escovitch (page 70).

INGREDIENTS

2 ½ PINTS (500 G) BRUSSELS SPROUTS, CLEANED, TRIMMED, AND HALVED

2 CLOVES GARLIC, MINCED

⅓ CUP (73 G) COCONUT OIL

2 TABLESPOONS (ABOUT 24 G) MARLEY COFFEE SPICE BLEND (PAGE 14)

KOSHER SALT AND FRESHLY GROUND BLACK PEPPER TO TASTE

DIRECTIONS

Preheat the oven to 375°F (190°C, or gas mark 5). In a large bowl, toss the Brussels sprouts with the garlic, coconut oil, Marley Coffee Spice Blend, salt, and pepper. Spread them evenly on a parchment paper–lined baking sheet. Roast for 20 minutes, stirring occasionally, or until the sprouts are golden brown and fork-tender.

TIP: CHOOSE BRIGHT GREEN BRUSSELS SPROUTS WITH COMPACT HEADS, AND KEEP THEM REFRIGERATED IN AN AIRTIGHT PLASTIC BAG FOR NO LONGER THAN 3 DAYS.

CHINESE-SPICED
❧ VEGETABLES AND TOFU ❧

YIELD: 4 SERVINGS

Brewed coffee along with chili paste and hoisin sauce enliven the flavor of this pretty, healthy vegetarian main course—which is likely to become your go-to dish when cooking for those who don't eat meat.

INGREDIENTS

3 TABLESPOONS (45 ML) SESAME OIL

1 TABLESPOON MINCED FRESH GINGER

1 CLOVE GARLIC, MINCED

2 HEADS BOK CHOY, WASHED, TRIMMED, AND ROUGHLY CHOPPED

2 HEADS BROCCOLI, CUT INTO FLORETS

1 (15-OUNCE, OR 425 G) CAN BABY CORN, DRAINED

¼ POUND (115 G) SHIITAKE MUSHROOMS, TRIMMED AND SLICED

1 GREEN BELL PEPPER, CORED, SEEDED, AND DICED SMALL
   (½ INCH, OR 1 CM)

1 LARGE CARROT, JULIENNED

¼ YELLOW ONION, DICED

1 BUNCH SCALLIONS (WHITE AND LIGHT GREEN PARTS),
   SLICED THIN, DIVIDED

⅓ CUP (80 ML) BREWED ONE LOVE COFFEE

¼ CUP (60 ML) LOW-SODIUM SOY SAUCE

¼ CUP (60 ML) VEGETABLE STOCK OR BROTH

2 TABLESPOONS (31 G) HOISIN SAUCE

1 TABLESPOON (15 G) CHILI PASTE

1 TABLESPOON (15 G) PACKED LIGHT BROWN SUGAR

2 TABLESPOONS (16 G) CORNSTARCH

1 (1-POUND, OR 454 G) PACKAGE FIRM TOFU, CUBED

DIRECTIONS

Preheat a large wok over medium heat for 2 minutes, or until very hot. Add the sesame oil and heat it for 1 minute, or until it shimmers. Add the ginger, garlic, bok choy, broccoli, baby corn, mushrooms, green pepper, carrot, onion, and half of the scallions. Stir-fry the vegetables for 5 to 6 minutes, or until the bok choy is wilted. Transfer to a large bowl and set aside.

Return the wok to medium heat. Add the coffee, soy sauce, vegetable stock, hoisin, chili paste, and brown sugar. Whisking constantly, bring the mixture to a rolling boil. Whisk in the cornstarch and continue to whisk until the sauce thickens, about 3 minutes. Return the vegetables to the wok and toss with the sauce.

Add the tofu and toss again. Transfer to a serving dish and garnish with the remaining scallions.

TIP: SERVE THIS COLORFUL, CRUNCHY DISH WITH WHITE RICE, IF DESIRED.

COCONUT-CURRY ROOT VEGETABLE STEW WITH A COFFEE BROTH

YIELD: 4 TO 6 SERVINGS AS A MAIN COURSE

Slightly exotic and beautifully colored thanks to the curry powder, coffee, and coconut milk, this hearty stew makes a fine vegetarian main course.

INGREDIENTS

¼ CUP (55 G) COCONUT OIL

1 YELLOW ONION, PEELED AND DICED

2 CLOVES GARLIC, MINCED

1 YUKON GOLD POTATO, PEELED AND DICED

1 VERY LARGE KABOCHA OR BUTTERNUT SQUASH,
   PEELED, SEEDED, AND CUT INTO 2-INCH (5 CM) CUBES

2 TABLESPOONS CHOPPED FRESH THYME LEAVES

1 LARGE CARROT, DICED

1 CUP (235 ML) COCONUT MILK

½ CUP (120 ML) VEGETABLE STOCK OR BROTH

½ CUP (120 ML) BREWED, COOLED ONE LOVE COFFEE

3 TABLESPOONS (19 G) CURRY POWDER

1 LEEK (WHITE AND LIGHT GREEN PARTS), CLEANED AND DICED

1 RED BELL PEPPER, CORED, SEEDED, AND SLICED THIN

1 HEAD CAULIFLOWER, CUT INTO FLORETS

3 TABLESPOONS CHOPPED FRESH ITALIAN PARSLEY

KOSHER SALT AND FRESHLY GROUND BLACK PEPPER TO TASTE

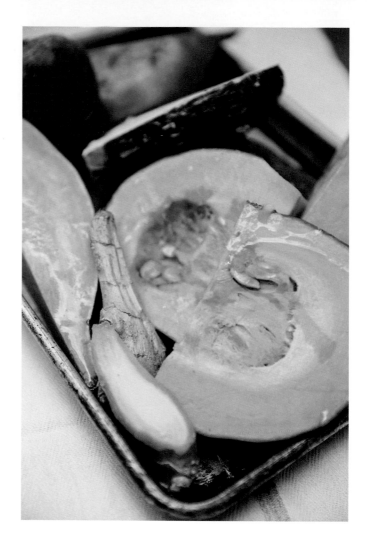

DIRECTIONS

In a large saucepan over medium heat, heat the coconut oil for 1 minute, or until very hot.

Add the onion, garlic, potato, and squash. Sauté for 5 minutes, stirring frequently, or until the onion is translucent. Add the thyme and cook for 2 or 3 minutes, stirring. Add the carrot and cook for 3 minutes more, stirring occasionally.

Stir in the coconut milk, vegetable stock, coffee, and curry powder. Reduce the heat to low and simmer for 25 minutes, stirring occasionally.

Add the leek, red bell pepper, cauliflower, and parsley. Simmer for 15 minutes more, or until the liquid is bubbling and the vegetables begin to soften. Taste and season with salt and pepper.

TIP: THIS IS NICE SERVED IN BOWLS WITH WHITE RICE, GARNISHED WITH FRESH HERBS OF YOUR CHOICE.

GRILLED VEGETABLE SKEWERS MARINATED IN COFFEE AND ❧ STAR ANISE–INFUSED OIL ❧

YIELD: 3 TO 4 SERVINGS

A lemony marinade made with our Coffee and Star Anise–Infused Oil (page 24) imparts a delicious flavor to these colorful vegetable skewers. Feel free to use whatever fresh vegetables you have on hand.

INGREDIENTS

FOR MARINADE:

¼ CUP (60 ML) COFFEE AND STAR ANISE-INFUSED OIL (PAGE 24)

2 CLOVES GARLIC, MINCED

JUICE OF 1 LEMON

1 BUNCH FRESH BASIL, TRIMMED AND CHOPPED

KOSHER SALT AND FRESHLY GROUND BLACK PEPPER TO TASTE

FOR VEGETABLES:

1 LARGE ZUCCHINI, ENDS REMOVED, CUT INTO 1-INCH (2.5 CM) PIECES

1 LARGE YELLOW SUMMER SQUASH, ENDS REMOVED, CUT INTO 1-INCH (2.5 CM) PIECES

1 LARGE RED ONION, CUT INTO 1-INCH (2.5 CM) PIECES

2 CUPS (298 G) CHERRY TOMATOES, STEMMED

1 CUP (96 G) BUTTON MUSHROOMS, STEM ENDS TRIMMED

1 RED BELL PEPPER, CORED, SEEDED, AND CUT INTO 1-INCH (2.5 CM) PIECES

2 EARS FRESH CORN, HUSKED AND CUT INTO THIRDS

DIRECTIONS

TO MAKE THE MARINADE:

In a small bowl, whisk the infused oil, garlic, lemon juice, and basil. Season with salt and pepper.

TO MAKE THE VEGETABLES:

Onto 6 to 8 metal skewers, thread the zucchini, yellow summer squash, red onion, cherry tomatoes, mushrooms, red bell pepper, and corn. Arrange the skewers on a large baking sheet. Brush with the marinade, making sure they are completely coated. Let marinate for 10 minutes. Reserve any remaining marinade.

Preheat a grill to medium or place a grill pan over medium heat. Place the skewers on a grill rack and place this on the grill, or place the skewers directly on the grill pan. Grill for 3 minutes. Brush the skewers with any remaining marinade. Grill for 3 minutes more, or until the vegetables begin to color and soften.

TIP: SERVE THESE WITH YOUR FAVORITE MEAT, OR ENJOY AS A HEALTHY VEGETARIAN MEAL OPTION.

LENTIL AND WHITE BEAN BURGERS FLAVORED ❧ WITH MARLEY COFFEE SPICE BLEND ❧

YIELD: 4 TO 6 BURGERS

You won't miss the meat in these flavor-packed burgers, which have both red lentils and white beans, along with Marley Coffee Spice Blend (page 14) for some extra kick.

INGREDIENTS

- 2 TABLESPOONS (28 G) UNSALTED BUTTER
- 6 TABLESPOONS (90 ML) EXTRA-VIRGIN OLIVE OIL, DIVIDED
- 1 SMALL YELLOW ONION, FINELY DICED
- 1 STALK CELERY, CHOPPED
- ½ LARGE CARROT, GRATED
- ¼ CUP CHOPPED FRESH CILANTRO LEAVES
- 2 CLOVES GARLIC, MINCED
- 2 (14-OUNCE, OR 395 G) CANS WHITE BEANS, RINSED AND DRAINED
- 1 (14-OUNCE, OR 395 G) CAN RED LENTILS, RINSED AND DRAINED
- 2 TABLESPOONS (30 ML) FRESHLY SQUEEZED LEMON JUICE
- ½ CUP (23 G) FRESH BREAD CRUMBS
- 1 TABLESPOON MAYONNAISE
- 1 EGG
- 2 TABLESPOONS (ABOUT 24 G) MARLEY COFFEE SPICE BLEND (PAGE 14)
- ¼ CUP (55 G) COCONUT OIL

DIRECTIONS

In a large skillet or sauté pan over medium heat, melt the butter with 3 tablespoons (45 ml) olive oil for 1 minute, or until very hot. Add the onion, celery, carrot, cilantro, and garlic. Cook for 2 to 3 minutes, or until the vegetables soften. Remove the pan from the heat and set aside.

In the work bowl of a food processor, combine the white beans, red lentils, lemon juice, and remaining 3 tablespoons (45 ml) olive oil. Pulse until the beans and lentils are fairly smooth. Transfer to a large bowl.

Stir in the bread crumbs, mayonnaise, egg, and Marley Coffee Spice Blend. Mix well. Add the sautéed vegetables. Shape the mixture into 4 to 6 patties of whatever size you prefer. Arrange the burgers on a parchment paper–lined baking sheet. Refrigerate for about 1 hour.

In a large skillet over medium heat, heat the coconut oil until very hot. Carefully place the burgers in the skillet and cook for about 3 minutes. With a large spatula, flip the burgers and continue to cook for 3 minutes more, or until steaming hot inside and crispy on the outside.

TIP: SERVE THESE BURGERS ON BURGER BUNS OR OPEN-FACED ON A SLICE OF TOAST.

HERB- AND GARLIC-ROASTED EGGPLANT WITH MARLEY COFFEE SPICE BLEND AND MOZZARELLA CHEESE

YIELD: 4 TO 6 SERVINGS

Eggplant can be a little bland on its own, but when marinated in garlic, basil, and lemon juice, plus Marley Coffee Spice Blend (page 14) and Coffee and Star Anise–Infused Oil (page 24), it becomes incredibly flavorful. This is definitely hearty enough to be a main course, thanks to the generous amount of cheese.

INGREDIENTS

2 CLOVES GARLIC, MINCED

1 BUNCH FRESH BASIL, STEMMED AND TORN INTO PIECES, (¼ CUP, OR ABOUT 9 G, RESERVED FOR GARNISH)

3 TABLESPOONS (ABOUT 36 G) MARLEY COFFEE SPICE BLEND (PAGE 14)

JUICE OF 1 LEMON

¼ CUP (60 ML) COFFEE AND STAR ANISE-INFUSED OIL (PAGE 24)

3 EGGPLANT, SLICED ABOUT ½-INCH (1 CM) THICK LENGTHWISE

1 CUP (235 ML) MARINARA SAUCE

1 POUND (454 G) MOZZARELLA CHEESE, SLICED ABOUT ½-INCH (1 CM) THICK

GRATED PARMESAN CHEESE, FOR GARNISH

DIRECTIONS

Preheat the oven to 375°F (190°C, or gas mark 5). In a medium-size bowl, whisk the garlic, basil (except the ¼ cup reserved for the garnish), Marley Coffee Spice Blend, lemon juice, and infused oil.

Arrange the eggplant in a single layer in a shallow roasting pan. Cut slits in each slice of eggplant. Evenly spoon the garlic and basil mixture over the slices. Roast for 20 minutes, turning once, or until fork-tender. Evenly spoon marinara sauce over each piece of eggplant. Top with mozzarella slices.

Preheat the broiler to low. Broil the eggplant for 3 to 4 minutes, or until golden brown. Garnish with the reserved basil and a sprinkle of Parmesan cheese.

NOTE: Fresh basil will keep, well wrapped in slightly damp paper towels and stored in a plastic bag, for up to 4 days in the refrigerator.

❧ ROASTED ROOT VEGETABLES ❧

YIELD: 8 SERVINGS

When coffee is finely ground and paired with sweet-smelling pumpkin pie spice, aromatic fresh rosemary, a drizzle of olive oil, and a small scoop of dark brown sugar, an inimitable marinade results. Tossed with vegetables, this marinade imparts a deep, deliciously caramelized flavor. Enjoy this dish with roast chicken or pork, or serve as a side dish or main course.

INGREDIENTS

6 LARGE CARROTS, DICED

6 GOLDEN BEETS, PEELED AND DICED

6 TURNIPS, PEELED AND DICED

3 CASSAVA, PEELED AND DICED

2 LARGE BUTTERNUT SQUASH, PEELED, SEEDED, AND DICED

¼ CUP (60 ML) EXTRA-VIRGIN OLIVE OIL

¼ CUP (60 G) PACKED DARK BROWN SUGAR

1 TABLESPOON PUMPKIN PIE SPICE

1 TEASPOON VERY FINELY GROUND ONE LOVE COFFEE BEANS

3 SPRIGS FRESH ROSEMARY, LEAVES STRIPPED AND CHOPPED

DIRECTIONS

Preheat the oven to 375° F (190°C, or gas mark 5). In a large bowl, toss together the carrots, beets, turnips, cassava, and butternut squash. Add the olive oil, brown sugar, pumpkin pie spice, coffee, and rosemary. Toss to combine. Transfer to a large rimmed baking sheet and roast for about 25 minutes, stirring occasionally, or until fork-tender.

NOTE: Cassava is a tuber with a tough brown skin and creamy white interior. Choose firm ones, and store in a cool, dark place for up to 1 week.

I CHOSE THE NAME, ONE LOVE, FOR THIS COFFEE BECAUSE "ONE LOVE" WAS ONE OF MY FATHER'S BIGGEST SONGS. LIKE JAMAICA, WHICH HAS CHINESE, EUROPEAN, AND ETHIOPIAN PEOPLE, THIS COFFEE IS A MELTING POT OF FLAVORS. I LOVE IT BECAUSE YOU CAN REALLY TASTE THE EARTH TONES, AND IT HAS GOOD BALANCE AND ACIDITY. ONE LOVE COFFEE GOES WELL WITH ETHIOPIAN, INDIAN, AND CHINESE FOOD.

ONE
LOVE

COFFEE-INFUSED ROASTED VEGETABLE AND KIDNEY BEAN ENCHILADAS ❧ WITH MOLE SAUCE ❧

YIELD: 6 ENCHILADAS

A nontraditional take on a Mexican classic, this dish features veggie-stuffed tortillas in a wonderful mole sauce burnished by One Love coffee. Try it when you have a craving for south-of-the-border fare!

INGREDIENTS

2 TABLESPOONS (30 ML) EXTRA-VIRGIN OLIVE OIL

2 SMALL TO MEDIUM-SIZE ZUCCHINI, ENDS TRIMMED, DICED

2 SMALL TO MEDIUM-SIZE YELLOW SUMMER SQUASH, ENDS TRIMMED, DICED

1 MEDIUM-SIZE RED ONION, DICED

1 RED BELL PEPPER, CORED, SEEDED, AND DICED

1 CLOVE GARLIC, MINCED

¼ BUNCH FRESH CILANTRO, STEMMED AND CHOPPED

1 (8-OUNCE, OR 225 G) CAN WHITE BEANS, RINSED AND DRAINED

½ TEASPOON GROUND WHITE PEPPER

KOSHER SALT TO TASTE

JUICE OF ½ LEMON

1 BATCH MOLE SAUCE (PAGE 87)

6 LARGE CORN TORTILLAS

2 CUPS (240 G) GRATED MONTEREY JACK CHEESE

2 SCALLIONS (WHITE AND LIGHT GREEN PARTS), SLICED THIN

2 CUPS (400 G) COOKED BROWN RICE

½ CUP (60 G) SOUR CREAM

1 LARGE RED RADISH, SLICED THIN

DIRECTIONS

Preheat the oven to 350°F (180°C, or gas mark 4).

Preheat a medium-size skillet or sauté pan over medium heat. Add the olive oil and, when it is very hot, add the zucchini, summer squash, red onion, red bell pepper, garlic, and cilantro. Sauté for about 2 minutes, or until the vegetables begin to soften. Stir in the white beans, white pepper, salt, and lemon juice. Remove from the heat and set aside.

Cover the bottom of a large baking pan with a layer of mole sauce. Place 1 tortilla on a clean work surface and place some sautéed vegetables in the center. Roll the tortilla and place it in the baking pan seam-side down. Repeat with the remaining tortillas and vegetables, until all of the tortillas are filled and arranged in a single layer in the pan. Top with mole sauce, Jack cheese, and scallions. Bake for 25 minutes, or until bubbly and hot. Serve with the brown rice and garnish with sour cream and radish slices.

❧ MOLE SAUCE ❧

Definitely seek out pasilla chillies for this mole, as they are especially good to use in sauces. They're medium-hot, richly flavored, and a blackish-brown color.

INGREDIENTS

2 CLOVES GARLIC, MINCED

1 SCALLION (WHITE AND LIGHT GREEN PARTS), SLICED THIN

1 PASILLA CHILLI, SEEDED AND CHOPPED

1 TABLESPOON (15 ML) EXTRA-VIRGIN OLIVE OIL

2 CUPS (458 G) CANNED BLACK BEANS, RINSED AND DRAINED

½ CUP (120 ML) CHICKEN STOCK OR BROTH

¼ CUP (60 ML) BREWED ONE LOVE COFFEE

2 TABLESPOONS GROUND CUMIN

2 TABLESPOONS (26 G) SUGAR

1 TABLESPOON CHILI POWDER

¼ CUP (44 G) CHOPPED DARK CHOCOLATE

DIRECTIONS

In a medium-size saucepan over medium heat, sauté the garlic, scallion, and chilli in the olive oil for about 2 minutes, or until the garlic starts to color. Add the black beans, chicken stock, coffee, cumin, sugar, and chili powder. Bring to a boil. Remove from the heat and carefully pour the mixture into a food processor. Blend until very smooth. Return the mixture to the saucepan. Bring to a simmer. Whisk in the chocolate until it melts and the mole is smooth. Set aside until ready to use.

COFFEE-SPICED VEGETABLE TACOS

YIELD: 6 TACOS

The vegetables for this fun, casual dish are spiked with cumin and Marley Coffee Spice Blend (page 14), sautéed, and stuffed into warm corn tortillas. The accompanying crunchy, colorful slaw contains yucca in addition to cabbage and carrot.

INGREDIENTS

FOR SLAW:

1 CUP (70 G) THINLY SLICED PURPLE CABBAGE

½ YUCCA, CUT INTO VERY THIN STRIPS

1 CARROT, CUT INTO VERY THIN STRIPS

¼ CUP (60 ML) EXTRA-VIRGIN OLIVE OIL

JUICE OF 1 LIME

1 TEASPOON AGAVE NECTAR

FOR TACOS:

¼ CUP (60 ML) EXTRA-VIRGIN OLIVE OIL, PLUS MORE FOR BRUSHING THE GRILL PAN

1 ZUCCHINI, ENDS TRIMMED, SLICED

1 YELLOW SUMMER SQUASH, ENDS REMOVED, SLICED

2 EARS FRESH CORN, HUSKED, KERNELS SCRAPED FROM THE COB, COBS DISCARDED

¼ MEDIUM-SIZE ONION, CHOPPED

1 CLOVE GARLIC, MINCED

1 BUNCH KALE, CLEANED AND CHOPPED

1 GREEN BELL PEPPER, CORED, SEEDED, AND DICED

½ BUNCH FRESH CILANTRO, STEMMED AND CHOPPED

1 TABLESPOON MARLEY COFFEE SPICE BLEND (PAGE 14)

1 TEASPOON GROUND CUMIN

KOSHER SALT AND FRESHLY GROUND BLACK PEPPER TO TASTE

6 CORN TORTILLA SHELLS

FOR GARNISH:

QUESO FRESCO, SOUR CREAM, FRESH CILANTRO LEAVES, AND LIME WEDGES

GRILLED OR ROASTED SCALLIONS (OPTIONAL)

DIRECTIONS

TO MAKE THE SLAW:

In a large glass bowl, toss together the cabbage, yucca, and carrot. Add the olive oil, lime juice, and agave nectar. Toss again until all ingredients are well mixed. Cover and refrigerate.

TO MAKE THE TACOS:

In a medium-size skillet or sauté pan over medium heat, heat the olive oil for 1 minute. Add the zucchini, summer squash, corn, onion, garlic, kale, green bell pepper, cilantro, Marley Coffee Spice Blend, cumin, salt, and pepper. Sauté for 2 minutes.

Preheat a grill pan over medium heat for 1 minute. Brush the pan with olive oil. Place the tortilla shells on the pan for 1 minute, or until very warm. Transfer to a serving platter and fill with sautéed vegetables. Top with slaw. Garnish with queso fresco, sour cream, cilantro, lime, and, if desired, grilled or roasted scallions.

NOTE: Queso fresco is a widely available Mexican cheese. If you can't find it, substitute your favorite cheese.

CHAPTER

5

HOT OFF THE GRILL

(Catch a Fire coffee)

Whatever you're grilling, coffee can boost the flavor—in particular, a coffee that features dark chocolaty notes and a subtle heat reminiscent of chilli peppers. Full-bodied and bold, Catch a Fire, for instance, stands up well to the intense heat of the grill, and is equally great on meat, fish, and assorted vegetables. Finely ground beans provide an earthy complexity to rubs, which can be used with ribs, steaks, and chicken.

When grilling, watch foods closely so they don't overcook. You can always return an underdone steak to the flame, but if it's overdone, there's no going back. Also, try something a little unexpected on your grill: In place of beef burgers, substitute grilled lamb burgers topped with a creamy mint and cucumber-infused sauce. Think fruit, like peaches and pears. Ripe peaches, for instance, take on a mahogany sheen and deep, sweet flavor when marinated in fresh herbs, brown sugar, and coffee. And instead of plain grilled chicken, slather quartered chickens before cooking with a mixture of barbecue sauce, brewed coffee, honey, and freshly grated orange zest and they will come off your grill caramelized and with just the right balance of sweet and spicy. With grilling, the possibilities are infinite. Rain or shine, hot or cold, let's get grilling!

HERB- AND COFFEE-GRILLED
❧ RIB EYE STEAKS ❧

YIELD: 4 SERVINGS

Choose the best steaks you can for this sumptuous dish. These flavorful steaks just get better when rubbed with a coffee bean–infused spice blend before cooking. Fresh garlic and rosemary only enhance the taste further.

INGREDIENTS

4 (8-OUNCE, OR 225 G) RIB EYE STEAKS

3 TABLESPOONS (ABOUT 36 G) MARLEY COFFEE SPICE BLEND (PAGE 14)

2 SPRIGS FRESH ROSEMARY, LEAVES STRIPPED AND CHOPPED

1 TABLESPOON (15 ML) EXTRA-VIRGIN OLIVE OIL

2 CLOVES GARLIC, PEELED

KOSHER SALT AND FRESHLY GROUND BLACK PEPPER TO TASTE

1 LEMON, ZESTED AND JUICED

DIRECTIONS

Preheat a charcoal grill to medium. Arrange the steaks on a large baking sheet. Rub them all over with the Marley Coffee Spice Blend. Sprinkle with rosemary. Rub with a little olive oil and the garlic. Season the steaks on both sides with salt and pepper. Sprinkle with some lemon juice and lemon zest. Refrigerate the steaks until the grill is nice and hot.

Grill the steaks: 5 minutes for medium-rare, 10 minutes for medium, or until they reach your desired doneness.

NOTE: While a charcoal grill imparts the best flavor to these steaks, you can use a grill pan with sizzlingly good results, too.

✦ BARBECUED COFFEE CHICKEN SKEWERS ✦

YIELD: 4 TO 6 SERVINGS

A full-bodied coffee contributes delicious flavor to the marinade for these addictive chicken bites, and it perfectly complements the herbs and barbecue sauce. Serve this as a main course or appetizer, and factor in time for soaking the wooden skewers before threading on the chicken.

INGREDIENTS

2 CLOVES GARLIC, MINCED

2 TABLESPOONS ONION POWDER

½ BUNCH FRESH CILANTRO, STEMMED AND CHOPPED

2 TABLESPOONS VERY FINELY GROUND CATCH A FIRE
COFFEE BEANS

JUICE OF 2 LIMES

KOSHER SALT AND FRESHLY GROUND BLACK PEPPER TO TASTE

2 POUNDS (908 G) BONELESS, SKINLESS CHICKEN THIGHS,
CUT INTO 1-INCH (2.5 CM) CHUNKS

2 CUPS (500 G) BARBECUE SAUCE

LIME WEDGES, FOR GARNISH

DIRECTIONS

Preheat the oven to 350°F (180°C, or gas mark 4). Soak 6 to 8 wooden skewers in water for 30 minutes. Alternatively, use metal skewers if that is what you have.

In a large bowl, stir together the garlic, onion powder, cilantro, coffee, lime juice, salt, and pepper. Add the chicken and stir to coat well with the marinade. Refrigerate, covered, for 1 hour. Thread 4 to 6 pieces of chicken onto each skewer.

Preheat a large grill pan over medium heat. Grill the skewers for about 3 minutes. Turn and grill the other side for about 5 minutes more, or until cooked through. You can do this in several batches.

Transfer the skewers to a large baking pan or rimmed baking sheet. Brush the chicken with the barbecue sauce. Bake for about 5 minutes, or until the sauce is caramelized. Serve the chicken with the lime wedges.

TIP: MAKE THIS DISH ON YOUR OUTDOOR GRILL IF YOU PREFER.

GRILLED PEACHES WITH COFFEE

YIELD: 4 SERVINGS

To add a dash of liveliness to these sweet grilled peaches, a deep, rich coffee is ideal. The flavor in this dish is further enlivened by cinnamon and thyme. Use only perfectly ripe peaches for this delectable dish.

INGREDIENTS

½ CUP (120 ML) BREWED CATCH A FIRE COFFEE

¼ CUP (60 G) PACKED LIGHT BROWN SUGAR

2 TABLESPOONS COCONUT OIL

2 TABLESPOONS CHOPPED FRESH THYME LEAVES

1 TABLESPOON GROUND CINNAMON

4 LARGE PEACHES, HALVED AND PITTED

DIRECTIONS

In a large bowl, whisk the coffee, brown sugar, coconut oil, thyme, and cinnamon until emulsified. Toss the peaches with this marinade and let marinate at room temperature for 1 hour, or overnight in the refrigerator.

Preheat a charcoal grill to medium or place a grill pan over medium heat. Place the peach halves on the grill for about 2 minutes per side, or until they soften and develop grill marks.

TIP: THESE PEACHES ARE EXCELLENT PAIRED WITH ANY GRILLED MEATS, BUT ARE ESPECIALLY DELICIOUS WITH RIBS OR BARBECUED COFFEE CHICKEN SKEWERS (PAGE 93).

GRILLED LAMB BURGERS SEASONED ❧ WITH MARLEY COFFEE SPICE BLEND ❧

YIELD: 4 BURGERS

Ground lamb, when spiked with Marley Coffee Spice Blend (page 14), garlic, and lemon, makes for a deliciously different burger. Whether you opt to serve these burgers in brioche buns or not, you'll want to whip up the accompanying cucumber sauce to go with them.

INGREDIENTS

FOR BURGERS:

2 POUNDS (908 G) GROUND LAMB

1 BUNCH FRESH PARSLEY, STEMMED AND CHOPPED

3 CLOVES GARLIC, MINCED

2 SHALLOTS, MINCED

GRATED ZEST OF 1 LEMON

1 EGG, LIGHTLY BEATEN

2 TABLESPOONS (ABOUT 24 G) MARLEY COFFEE SPICE BLEND (PAGE 14)

FOR CUCUMBER SAUCE:

½ CUCUMBER, PEELED AND DICED

1 CLOVE GARLIC, MINCED

1 YELLOW ONION, MINCED

½ CUP (115 G) SOUR CREAM

¼ CUP (60 G) MAYONNAISE

1 TABLESPOON CHOPPED FRESH MINT

KOSHER SALT AND FRESHLY GROUND BLACK PEPPER TO TASTE

4 BRIOCHE BUNS, OR BREAD OF CHOICE

BUTTER LETTUCE, FOR SERVING

RED ONIONS, CHOPPED, FOR GARNISH (OPTIONAL)

DIRECTIONS

TO MAKE THE LAMB BURGERS:

In a large bowl, combine the lamb, parsley, garlic, shallot, lemon zest, egg, and Marley Coffee Spice Blend. Mix lightly with your hands. Form into 4 patties.

Preheat a large grill pan over medium heat. Grill the patties for about 6 minutes per side, or until done. They will be firm to the touch.

TO MAKE THE CUCUMBER SAUCE:

In a medium-size bowl, whisk the cucumber, garlic, onion, sour cream, mayonnaise, and mint. Add salt and pepper to taste.

When the burgers are done, place them in the buns. Top each with cucumber sauce and butter lettuce. Garnish with red onion, if desired.

TIP: IF YOU LIKE YOUR BURGERS MORE WELL-DONE, PLACE THEM IN A PREHEATED 400°F (200°C, OR GAS MARK 6) OVEN FOR ABOUT 5 MINUTES AFTER GRILLING THEM.

GRILLED SWEET POTATOES
❖ WITH ROSEMARY-COFFEE-HONEY GLAZE ❖

YIELD: **4 SERVINGS**

Catch a Fire coffee is the ideal ingredient in a glaze. Here, it tempers the honey's sweetness and the garlic and rosemary lend added dimensions of flavor.

INGREDIENTS

¾ CUP (255 G) HONEY

¼ CUP (60 ML) BREWED, COOLED CATCH A FIRE COFFEE

2 CLOVES GARLIC, MINCED

2 SPRIGS FRESH ROSEMARY, LEAVES STRIPPED AND CHOPPED

3 SWEET POTATOES, CUT INTO THICK WEDGES

¼ CUP (55 G) COCONUT OIL

DIRECTIONS

In a large saucepan over medium heat, stir together the honey, coffee, garlic, and rosemary. Bring to a simmer, reduce the heat to low, and cook for 3 to 4 minutes, or until well blended and smooth.

Meanwhile, preheat a grill to medium or place a grill pan over medium heat.

In a large bowl, toss the sweet potato wedges with the coconut oil. When all wedges have a nice shine, transfer them to the grill. Grill for about 5 minutes per side, turning once. When fork-tender, remove them from the grill. Ladle the glaze over the sweet potatoes before serving.

NOTE: When you buy sweet potatoes, look for small to medium-size ones with unbruised skins, and store them in a dry, dark spot—but not the refrigerator. Sweet potatoes will keep for a couple of weeks at room temperature.

ROSEMARY- AND COFFEE-SPICED
❧ GRILLED LAMB CHOPS ❧

YIELD: 4 SERVINGS

Allow at least 45 minutes for the lamb chops to marinate so they pick up the fresh, sassy flavors of the coffee, balsamic vinegar, and lemon juice. Serve with your favorite vegetable and a big green salad.

INGREDIENTS

¼ CUP (60 ML) EXTRA-VIRGIN OLIVE OIL

¼ CUP (60 ML) BREWED CATCH A FIRE COFFEE

¼ CUP (60 ML) BALSAMIC VINEGAR

JUICE OF ½ LEMON

3 SPRIGS FRESH ROSEMARY, LEAVES STRIPPED AND CHOPPED

2 CLOVES GARLIC, MINCED

2 ½ POUNDS (1.13 KG) LAMB CHOPS

DIRECTIONS

In a bowl large enough to hold all the chops, whisk the olive oil, coffee, balsamic vinegar, lemon juice, rosemary, and garlic. Add the chops and toss to coat. Cover, refrigerate, and let marinate for 45 minutes, or overnight.

Preheat a grill to medium. Remove the chops from the marinade and place them on the grill about 6 inches (15 cm) from the heat source. Grill for 5 minutes per side, or until they reach your desired doneness. Let rest for about 10 minutes before serving to lock in the juices.

NOTE: You can use domestic or imported (from New Zealand) lamb chops with equal success in this dish.

❧ GRILLED VEGETABLE PANINI ❧

YIELD: 4 SERVINGS

The marinade for this delicious meatless dish contains a splash of Catch a Fire coffee, which brightens the vegetables destined for the grill. Whole-grain ciabatta is the top choice for these hefty sandwiches, but feel free to use your favorite whole-wheat rolls. And if you like other vegetables better, feel free to substitute them!

INGREDIENTS

½ CUP (120 ML) EXTRA-VIRGIN OLIVE OIL, PLUS MORE FOR OILING THE GRILL

¼ CUP (60 ML) BALSAMIC VINEGAR

3 TABLESPOONS (45 ML) BREWED, COOLED CATCH A FIRE COFFEE

2 CLOVES GARLIC, MINCED

KOSHER SALT AND FRESHLY GROUND BLACK PEPPER TO TASTE

1 ZUCCHINI, ENDS TRIMMED, SLICED INTO ½-INCH (1 CM) ROUNDS

1 SUMMER SQUASH, ENDS TRIMMED, SLICED INTO ½-INCH (1 CM) ROUNDS

1 RED BELL PEPPER, CORED, SEEDED, AND SLICED INTO ½-INCH (1 CM) STRIPS

1 RED ONION, SLICED THIN

1 BUNCH ASPARAGUS, ENDS TRIMMED

2 WHOLE PORTOBELLO MUSHROOMS, TRIMMED AND HALVED OR SLICED

3 TABLESPOONS (ABOUT 36 G) MARLEY COFFEE SPICE BLEND (PAGE 14)

4 WHOLE-GRAIN CIABATTA ROLLS, 8 SLICES WHOLE-GRAIN BREAD, OR 1 LONG CIABATTA LOAF, HALVED LENGTHWISE

BUTTER

8 SLICES HAVARTI CHEESE

DIRECTIONS

In a large bowl, whisk the olive oil, balsamic vinegar, coffee, garlic, salt, and pepper. Add the zucchini, summer squash, red bell pepper, red onion, asparagus, and portobellos, tossing with the marinade so they are well coated.

Preheat a grill to medium or place a grill pan over medium heat. Brush the grill with a little olive oil. Arrange the vegetables on the grill and sprinkle with the Marley Coffee Spice Blend. Grill the vegetables for 2 minutes, or until they begin to color. Turn the vegetables and grill for 5 minutes more, or until they start to soften and color. Transfer the grilled vegetables to a large plate and cover with aluminum foil to keep warm.

Arrange the bottom halves of the rolls or bread on a cutting board. Butter the outer side of each one. Fill with grilled vegetables, top with cheese, and cover with the bun tops.

Place the sandwiches on the grill and top with a cast iron skillet or a foil-wrapped brick to compress the sandwiches. Grill for 3 to 5 minutes, or until the cheese melts and the bread develops nice grill marks.

I AM A HUGE COFFEE DRINKER. WHEN I WAS YOUNGER, I DRANK A LOT OF COFFEE, TOO, BUT I DIDN'T KNOW IT HAD SO MANY NOTES, SO MANY FLAVORS. I HAD NO IDEA THERE WERE SO MANY VARIETIES OF COFFEE. I ESPECIALLY LIKE JAMAICAN COFFEE BECAUSE IT HAS SUCH A BALANCED ACIDITY. NOW THAT I AM MORE KNOWLEDGEABLE ABOUT COFFEE, IF I EVEN CHANGE UP THE WATER I USE TO MAKE IT, I CAN TASTE THE DIFFERENCE.

FIRE-ROASTED CORN WITH COFFEE AND ❧ HERB BUTTER ❧

YIELD: 4 SERVINGS

There's nothing like the taste of freshly grilled corn and, when topped with this expertly seasoned butter, it becomes even more of a delight. Make this awesome dish when corn and basil are at their best. You might want to double the recipe—it's doubtful you will have any leftovers.

INGREDIENTS

4 EARS FRESH CORN, HUSKS PEELED BACK OR REMOVED COMPLETELY

4 TEASPOONS (18 G) COCONUT OIL

KOSHER SALT TO TASTE

½ POUND (2 STICKS, OR 225 G) UNSALTED BUTTER, SOFTENED

2 TABLESPOONS (ABOUT 24 G) MARLEY COFFEE SPICE BLEND (PAGE 14)

1 BUNCH FRESH BASIL, STEMMED AND CHOPPED

2 CLOVES GARLIC, MINCED

1 TEASPOON BLACK SEA SALT

½ CUP (59 G) QUESO FRESCO

¼ BUNCH FRESH CILANTRO, STEMMED AND CHOPPED

DIRECTIONS

Preheat a grill to medium. Brush the corn with coconut oil and season it with kosher salt. Grill the corn for about 4 minutes per side, or until nicely charred and fully cooked.

Meanwhile, in a small bowl, blend the butter, Marley Coffee Spice Blend, basil, garlic, and black sea salt. Brush or spoon the seasoned butter onto the corn. Top with queso fresco and cilantro.

NOTE: Look for corn that has snugly fitting, bright to pale green husks, and golden to light brown silk. It's best to cook and serve fresh corn the day you buy it, but you can store it in the refrigerator for a day.

MARLEY SIGNATURE JERK CHICKEN

YIELD: 6 TO 8 SERVINGS

This Jamaican classic is a (tropical) breeze to make. Homemade jerk seasoning is rubbed under the skin of the bird, imparting Caribbean notes. The chicken is first grilled and finished in the oven so it doesn't become overcooked. Make plenty of this chicken as it disappears quickly.

INGREDIENTS

¼ CUP (ABOUT 54 G) JERK SEASONING (PAGE 17), PLUS MORE FOR SEASONING THE CHICKEN

1 TABLESPOON MARLEY COFFEE SPICE BLEND (PAGE 14)

¼ CUP (55 G) COCONUT OIL, PLUS MORE FOR RUBBING THE CHICKEN

2 (3-POUND, OR 1.36 KG) WHOLE CHICKENS, QUARTERED

KOSHER SALT AND FRESHLY GROUND BLACK PEPPER TO TASTE

LIME WEDGES, FOR GARNISH (OPTIONAL)

DIRECTIONS

In a small bowl, mix the jerk seasoning, Marley Coffee Spice Blend, and coconut oil. Loosen the skin on the chickens' breasts and backs, and rub some seasoning mixture under the skin. Sprinkle additional jerk seasoning all over the chicken. Season with salt and pepper. Refrigerate the chicken, loosely covered, for 45 minutes, or overnight.

Preheat a grill to medium or place a grill pan over medium heat. Preheat the oven to 350°F (180°C, or gas mark 4). Rub the chicken with a little coconut oil.

• If you are using a grill, grill the chicken for 45 minutes, turning occasionally. Transfer it to a baking pan and bake for 15 minutes, or until cooked to an internal temperature of 165°F (74°C), measured with a meat thermometer.

• If you are using a grill pan, grill the chicken for 5 minutes, or until nicely colored. Transfer it to the oven and bake for 1 hour, or until cooked to an internal temperature of 165°F (74°C), measured with a meat thermometer.

Serve, garnished with lime wedges if desired.

GRILLED HONEY-GLAZED CHICKEN

YIELD: 4 TO 6 SERVINGS

The coffee's dark chocolate notes harmonize with the honey and barbecue sauce to create an unforgettable glaze for this chicken. The glaze imparts deep flavor and the heat of the chile peppers in the coffee is a perfect accent.

INGREDIENTS

2 (3-POUND, OR 1.36 KG) WHOLE CHICKENS, QUARTERED

1 TABLESPOON MARLEY COFFEE SPICE BLEND (PAGE 14)

JUICE OF 1 ORANGE

3 CLOVES GARLIC, MINCED

2 TABLESPOONS CHOPPED FRESH THYME LEAVES

2 CUPS (500 G) COFFEE-SPICED BARBECUE SAUCE (PAGE 16)

¼ CUP (60 ML) BREWED, COOLED CATCH A FIRE COFFEE

¼ CUP (85 G) HONEY

GRATED ZEST OF 1 ORANGE

2 SCALLIONS (WHITE AND LIGHT GREEN PARTS), CHOPPED

DIRECTIONS

In a large bowl, combine the chicken, Marley Coffee Spice Blend, orange juice, garlic, and thyme. Toss to make sure all chicken pieces are evenly coated with the spice mixture. Cover and set aside to marinate for 25 minutes.

Preheat a charcoal grill to medium. Place the chicken, skin-side up, on the grill about 6 inches (15 cm) from the heat. Grill for 30 minutes. Flip and grill for 30 minutes more, or until the chicken is thoroughly cooked to an internal temperature of 165°F (74°C), measured with a meat thermometer. Keep an eye on the grill to make sure the fire isn't too high. Transfer the chicken to a large serving bowl.

Meanwhile, in another bowl, whisk the barbecue sauce, coffee, honey, orange zest, and scallions. Ladle the glaze over the chicken.

THIS RECIPE WORKS BEST WHEN YOU USE A CHARCOAL GRILL, BUT YOU CAN ALSO COOK THE CHICKEN ON A GAS GRILL, OR EVEN IN A GRILL PAN. IF YOU USE A GRILL PAN, GRILL THE CHICKEN FOR ABOUT 10 MINUTES, TURNING ONCE, AND FINISH COOKING IN A PREHEATED 350°F (180°C, OR GAS MARK 4) OVEN.

GRILLED SWORDFISH WITH
❧ BLACK BEAN AND TOMATO RELISH ❧

YIELD: 4 SERVINGS

Marley Coffee Spice Blend (page 14) brings out the best in fresh swordfish for a seafood dish that's irresistible, and the colorful relish heightens the flavor.

INGREDIENTS

FOR RELISH:

1 BEEFSTEAK TOMATO, DICED

1 SHALLOT, DICED

1 CLOVE GARLIC, MINCED

1 CUP (256 G) CANNED BLACK BEANS, RINSED AND DRAINED

¼ CUP (60 ML) EXTRA-VIRGIN OLIVE OIL

1 TABLESPOON (15 ML) COCONUT VINEGAR

1 TEASPOON SUGAR

1 TABLESPOON FRESH BASIL CHIFFONADE (SEE NOTE)

FOR FISH:

1 POUND (454 G) FRESH SWORDFISH, CUT ½ INCH (1 CM) THICK

1 TABLESPOON MARLEY COFFEE SPICE BLEND (PAGE 14)

KOSHER SALT AND FRESHLY GROUND BLACK PEPPER TO TASTE

JUICE OF ½ LEMON

2 TABLESPOONS (30 ML) EXTRA-VIRGIN OLIVE OIL

1 TABLESPOON CHOPPED FRESH PARSLEY

DIRECTIONS

TO MAKE THE RELISH:

In a medium-size bowl, gently stir together the tomato, shallot, garlic, and black beans. Sprinkle with the olive oil, coconut vinegar, and sugar. Toss gently to coat the vegetables. Sprinkle with the basil and set aside.

TO MAKE THE FISH:

Season the swordfish with the Marley Coffee Spice Blend, salt, and pepper. Sprinkle with lemon juice and olive oil.

Preheat a grill to medium. Grill the swordfish for about 3 minutes per side, or until it flakes easily with a fork. Transfer to a serving platter and garnish with the parsley. Serve with the relish.

NOTE: To cut an herb or vegetable into chiffonade means to slice it into shreds or strips. The easiest way to do this is with a pair of kitchen shears.

GRILLED SWORDFISH WITH COCONUT RICE AND TROPICAL CITRUS
❧ AND CILANTRO SALSA ❧

YIELD: 4 SERVINGS

Serve this appealing fish dish with chilled Coffee Stout (page 129) or another of our delicious cocktails (see chapter 6). If you like, substitute red snapper or grouper for the swordfish.

INGREDIENTS

FOR SWORDFISH:

JUICE OF 2 LIMES

JUICE OF 1 NAVEL ORANGE

JUICE OF 1 PINK GRAPEFRUIT

4 (6-OUNCE, OR 170 G) SWORDFISH STEAKS

1 TABLESPOON MARLEY COFFEE SPICE BLEND

SALT AND FRESHLY GROUND BLACK PEPPER TO TASTE

FOR RICE:

1 SPANISH ONION, DICED

2 TABLESPOONS (30 ML) VEGETABLE OIL

2 CUPS (370 G) UNCOOKED BASMATI RICE OR JASMINE RICE

3 CUPS (705 ML) UNSWEETENED COCONUT MILK

½ CUP (120 ML) WATER

½ CUP (43 G) TOASTED FLAKED COCONUT

FOR SALSA:

1 CUP (155 G) DICED PINEAPPLE

1 NAVEL ORANGE, SEGMENTED AND CUT INTO 1-INCH (2.5 CM) PIECES

1 PINK GRAPEFRUIT, SEGMENTED AND CUT INTO 1-INCH (2.5 CM) PIECES

¼ CUP CHOPPED FRESH CILANTRO LEAVES

2 CLOVES GARLIC, CHOPPED

2 TABLESPOONS (30 ML) CHAMPAGNE VINEGAR

1 TABLESPOON SUGAR

SALT AND FRESHLY GROUND BLACK PEPPER TO TASTE

FOR FRIED WONTONS:

6 SMALL WONTON SKINS, JULIENNED

2 CUPS (475 ML) VEGETABLE OIL, FOR FRYING THE WONTONS, PLUS MORE FOR THE GRILL PAN

DIRECTIONS

TO MAKE THE FISH:

In a small nonreactive bowl, combine the lime juice, orange juice, and grapefruit juice.

In a large, shallow glass pan, arrange the swordfish in a single layer. Pour the juice over the fish, turn to coat, and season with the Marley Coffee Spice Blend, salt, and pepper. Refrigerate the fish to marinate for 20 minutes.

MEANWHILE, TO MAKE THE RICE:

In a large skillet or sauté pan over high heat, cook the onion in the vegetable oil for about 3 minutes, or until translucent. Add the rice, stirring to coat the grains with the oil. Add the coconut milk, water, and coconut flakes. Stir once, cover, and cook over medium-low heat for 20 minutes, or until the mixture comes to a boil and steam starts to escape from the pan. Remove from the heat and set aside for at least 20 minutes, covered.

TO MAKE THE SALSA:

In a medium-size bowl, gently stir together the pineapple, orange, grapefruit, cilantro, garlic, champagne vinegar, and sugar. Taste and season with salt and pepper as desired. Cover and set aside.

TO MAKE THE FRIED WONTONS:

In a medium-size skillet over medium-high heat, heat the vegetable oil. Add the wonton strips and fry for 3 minutes, or until golden and crisp. Transfer to paper towels to drain.

Preheat a large grill pan over high heat. Brush it lightly with vegetable oil. Remove the fish from the marinade and place it in the grill pan. Grill for 3 to 4 minutes per side, or until done. It should reach an internal temperature of 150°F (65.5°C). Transfer the fish to a serving platter.

Fluff the rice with a fork and transfer it to a serving bowl. Season with salt and pepper as desired. Top the swordfish steaks with salsa, garnish with the fried wontons, and serve with the rice.

NOTE: When shopping for coconut milk for this dish, don't pick up cream of coconut by mistake. Canned coconut milk, widely available in supermarkets, is unsweetened, while cream of coconut (coconut cream) is sweetened and used mainly for desserts and mixed drinks.

CHAPTER

6

THIRST-QUENCHING SIPPERS AND CHILLERS

(Lively Up! coffee)

Pouring a dollop of liquor into a cup of coffee or espresso (and maybe topping it off with a cap of whipped cream) is certainly the perfect ending to a dinner. If the liquor is sweet, such as hazelnut-flavored liqueur or chocolate liqueur, the coffee can, basically, become dessert. But there's another way to enjoy the happy pairing of coffee and alcohol: in a cocktail.

The best coffee-based cocktails start with a liquor infused with coffee beans. In our drinks, we like to use Lively Up! coffee because of its deep, earthy flavor and notes of caramel and dark chocolate. Though this is a dark coffee, the acidity is unusually well balanced, making it the perfect variety to infuse into liquor. The infusion process is not difficult, but you will need to plan ahead because it takes anywhere from one day to two weeks. See page 120 for instructions.

From our roster of coffee-based drinks, there's a luscious martini made with four kinds of liqueur, a creamy sweet cognac-based drink, and a fruity concoction that features rum, tequila, passionfruit purée, and brewed, chilled coffee. And there are drinks that bear our names: The Rohan Marley (page 125), a blend of Galliano, tequila, and coffee garnished with grilled pineapple, and The Hardy 2 (page 122) made with bourbon, Grand Marnier, and a twist of orange peel. We hope you find a new favorite. They're all easy to make, and definitely party ready!

❖ ESPRESSO MARTINI ❖

YIELD: 1 SERVING

A whisper of light citrus, dark, rich espresso, and a combo of liqueurs make this martini sing. It's one of the prettiest drinks you'll ever shake, too.

INGREDIENTS

1 OR 2 ORANGE PEEL TWISTS

2 OUNCES (60 ML) ESPRESSO-VANILLA BEAN-INFUSED VODKA (PAGE 120)

1 OUNCE (30 ML) FRESHLY BREWED ESPRESSO

½ OUNCE (15 ML) ALMOND-FLAVORED LIQUEUR, SUCH AS AMARETTO

½ OUNCE (15 ML) HAZELNUT-FLAVORED LIQUEUR, SUCH AS FRANGELICO

½ OUNCE (15 ML) COFFEE-FLAVORED LIQUEUR, SUCH AS KAHLÚA

¼ OUNCE (5.5 ML) ORANGE-FLAVORED LIQUEUR, SUCH AS GRAND MARNIER

WHIPPED CREAM AND COCOA POWDER, OPTIONAL, FOR GARNISH

DIRECTIONS

Rim a martini glass with an orange peel twist and place it into the glass.

In a cocktail shaker, combine the infused vodka, espresso, almond-flavored liqueur, hazelnut-flavored liqueur, coffee-flavored liqueur, and orange-flavored liqueur. Stir very well. Add some ice, cover, and shake for 10 seconds. Strain into the martini glass. Garnish the glass with whipped cream and cocoa powder or the remaining orange peel twist, if desired.

NOTE: This recipe works well with espresso-vanilla bean–infused vodka, especially if you like a sweeter finish, but any espresso vodka or vanilla vodka will do.

❧ PARADISE PUNCH ❧

YIELD: 8 TO 10 SERVINGS

A felicitous blend of rum and fruit juices bolstered with chilled coffee, this is a beautiful drink to serve at a party. Mix up a batch beforehand and shake each guest's drink individually. If you're serving a thirsty crowd, double this recipe and keep one full pitcher of punch in the refrigerator until you need it.

INGREDIENTS

3 CUPS (705 ML) VANILLA, COCONUT, PINEAPPLE, BLACK CHERRY, OR PASSIONFRUIT RUM

1½ CUPS (12 OUNCES, OR 355 ML) FRESHLY SQUEEZED KEY LIME JUICE

1½ CUPS (12 OUNCES, OR 355 ML) PINEAPPLE JUICE

½ CUP (120 ML) BREWED, CHILLED LIVELY UP! COFFEE

¾ CUP (6 OUNCES, OR 175 ML) SIMPLE SYRUP (SEE TIP)

PINEAPPLE SLICES, PINEAPPLE LEAVES, LIME WEDGES, OR FRESH FRUIT OF YOUR CHOICE FOR GARNISH (OPTIONAL)

DIRECTIONS

In a large pitcher, stir together the rum, lime juice, pineapple juice, coffee, and simple syrup. Pour about 6 ounces (175 ml) into a cocktail shaker, add several ice cubes, cover, and shake vigorously for about 15 seconds. Strain into a highball glass over fresh ice cubes.

Repeat with the remaining punch.

Garnish each drink with a pineapple slice, pineapple leaf, lime wedge, or fresh fruit of your choice (if using).

TIP: TO MAKE A SIMPLE SYRUP, SIMPLY COOK EQUAL PARTS SUGAR AND WATER OVER LOW HEAT UNTIL CLEAR, THEN BOIL FOR 1 MINUTE, STIRRING.

❧ COFFEE INFUSIONS ❧

YIELD: 750 ML

Marley Coffee beans are strong and flavorful and, when you add them to liquor, the infusion process begins almost immediately. You'll want to let your infusing liquor sit for anywhere from one day (for a light taste with a whisper of coffee) to two weeks (at which point your liquor will have a dark, rich coffee flavor). Letting liquor infuse for too long may result in bitterness, so taste your infusion daily to see what "flavor profile" best suits your taste buds! And feel free to infuse whatever booze you like—rum, bourbon, and vodka are all favorites of ours.

INGREDIENTS

750 ML BOTTLE OF RUM, BOURBON, VODKA, OR YOUR PREFERRED LIQUOR

1 CUP (102 G) LIVELY UP! COFFEE BEANS

5 WHOLE VANILLA BEANS (OPTIONAL)

DIRECTIONS

Pour out 1 or 2 ounces (30 to 60 ml) from the 750-milliliter bottle of liquor.

Add the coffee beans to the bottle. For extra flavor, you also may add vanilla beans—use about five whole beans, sliced lengthwise, for each 750-milliliter bottle of liquor.

Cover the bottle and set aside. Don't forget to taste daily!

When the liquor has reached the desired potency, strain it and discard the coffee beans and vanilla beans. You will have a delicious infused liquor to enjoy.

❖ COFFEE-INFUSED OLD-FASHIONED ❖

YIELD: 1 SERVING

A traditional old-fashioned gets some extra kick from coffee liqueur as well as coffee-infused bourbon whiskey. Make this drink for friends who are extra special to you.

INGREDIENTS

2 OUNCES (60 ML) LIVELY UP! COFFEE-INFUSED BOURBON WHISKEY

9 DROPS ORANGE BITTERS

½ OUNCE (15 ML) COFFEE-FLAVORED LIQUEUR, SUCH AS KAHLÚA

ORANGE PEEL TWIST AND A LUXARDO CHERRY, FOR GARNISH

DIRECTIONS

In a rocks glass, stir together the infused bourbon whiskey, bitters, and coffee-flavored liqueur. Add a few ice cubes and briskly stir again. Garnish with an orange peel twist and the cherry.

NOTE: Luxardo cherries, produced in Luxardo, Italy, are worth finding for your cocktails, whether you're making Old-Fashioneds for the adults or Shirley Temples for the kids. These Marasca cherries preserved in the fruit's liqueur have a wonderful sweet-tart flavor and a dense texture.

❧ THE HARDY 2 ❧

YIELD: 1 SERVING

Simple to make, elegant to look at, and ultra-refreshing to drink, this is a cocktail you'll make again and again.

INGREDIENTS

2 OUNCES (60 ML) LIVELY UP! COFFEE-INFUSED BOURBON
(PAGE 120)

1 OUNCE (30 ML) ORANGE-FLAVORED LIQUEUR,
SUCH AS GRAND MARNIER

1 ORANGE PEEL TWIST, OPTIONAL

DIRECTIONS

In a cocktail shaker, combine the infused bourbon and orange-flavored liqueur. Add a few ice cubes. Cover and shake vigorously for 1 minute. Place a few ice cubes in a rocks or martini glass. Strain the cocktail into the glass. Garnish with the orange twist, if desired.

THIRST-QUENCHING SIPPERS AND CHILLERS

❧ COFFEE SUGAR ❧

YIELD: 1 SERVING

If you love your coffee light and sweet, this creamy cocktail is for you. Heavy cream and crème de cacao modulate the rich, dark, coffee-infused cognac, and a sprinkle of fresh nutmeg adds spiciness.

INGREDIENTS

FOR OPTIONAL GARNISH / RIM:

2 TEASPOONS SUGAR

¼ TEASPOON INSTANT COFFEE

FOR COCKTAIL:

1 OUNCE (30 ML) LIVELY UP! COFFEE-INFUSED COGNAC (PAGE 120)

1 OUNCE (30 ML) CRÈME DE CACAO

1 OUNCE (30 ML) HEAVY CREAM

½ OUNCE (15 ML) SIMPLE SYRUP

FRESHLY GRATED NUTMEG, FOR GARNISH

DIRECTIONS

TO MAKE THE GARNISH (IF USING):

On a small plate, mix the sugar and instant coffee. Coat the rim of a martini glass moistened with water with this mixture. Set the glass aside.

TO MAKE THE COCKTAIL:

In a cocktail shaker, combine the infused cognac, crème de cacao, heavy cream, and simple syrup. Cover and shake vigorously for 1 minute. Place a few ice cubes in a rocks glass. Strain the cocktail over the ice cubes. Garnish the drink with nutmeg.

TIP: REPLACE THE COGNAC WITH YOUR FAVORITE COFFEE-INFUSED BRANDY.

THE ROHAN MARLEY

YIELD: 1 SERVING

There's an amazing variety of flavors in this drink, from the delightful coffee-infused tequila and Galliano liqueur to the hints of chocolate, lemon, and pineapple. Somehow they all come together in a cocktail that is not only beautiful but refreshing.

INGREDIENTS

2 LARGE WEDGES GRILLED PINEAPPLE

2 OUNCES (60 ML) LIVELY UP! COFFEE-INFUSED TEQUILA (PAGE 120)

¾ OUNCE (22.5 ML) GALLIANO LIQUEUR

½ OUNCE (15 ML) CHOCOLATE SIMPLE SYRUP (SEE TIP)

¾ OUNCE (22.5 ML) MEYER LEMON JUICE

SMALL WEDGES FRESH PINEAPPLE, FOR GARNISH

NOTE: Meyer lemon juice, which is sweeter and more robustly flavored than regular lemon juice, is available in some specialty stores. If you can't find it, pick up some Meyer lemons and squeeze your own juice. In a pinch, use regular lemons.

DIRECTIONS

In a cocktail shaker, muddle the grilled pineapple wedges. Pour in the infused tequila, Galliano, chocolate simple syrup, and lemon juice. Cover and shake vigorously for about 20 seconds. Strain the mixture into a martini glass. Garnish with a wedge of fresh pineapple.

TIP: TO MAKE CHOCOLATE SIMPLE SYRUP: IN A SAUCEPAN OVER MEDIUM HEAT, COMBINE 1 CUP (235 ML) WATER AND 1 CUP (200 G) SUGAR, STIRRING, UNTIL THE SUGAR IS COMPLETELY DISSOLVED AND THE MIXTURE IS CLEAR. STIR IN ¼ CUP (22 G) ORGANIC COCOA POWDER AND MIX VERY WELL. LET THE SYRUP STAND UNTIL COOL; STRAIN. USE IMMEDIATELY OR REFRIGERATE IN A TIGHTLY COVERED CONTAINER.

JAMAICAN COFFEE BREEZE

YIELD: 1 SERVING

In the mood for a festive cocktail? This is your ticket to the fun. With a trio of fruit flavorings, plus dark rum, tequila, and a splash of cold coffee, it's like a Caribbean toast to sunny skies and balmy temperatures.

INGREDIENTS

1 OUNCE (30 ML) DARK JAMAICAN RUM, PREFERABLY MARLEY BRAND

1 OUNCE (30 ML) AÑEJO TEQUILA

1 OUNCE (30 ML) BREWED, CHILLED LIVELY UP! COFFEE

½ OUNCE (15 ML) PASSIONFRUIT PURÉE

½ OUNCE (15 ML) PINEAPPLE JUICE

½ OUNCE (15 ML) FRESHLY SQUEEZED LIME JUICE

½ OUNCE (15 ML) AGAVE NECTAR

PINEAPPLE LEAF, FOR GARNISH

DIRECTIONS

In a cocktail shaker, combine the rum, tequila, coffee, passionfruit purée, pineapple juice, lime juice, and agave nectar. Add a few ice cubes, cover, and shake vigorously for several seconds. Place a few ice cubes in a rocks glass. Strain the cocktail into the glass. Garnish with the pineapple leaf.

TIP: YOU MAY SUBSTITUTE HONEY FOR THE AGAVE NECTAR, AND ADD A LITTLE EXTRA IF YOU LIKE A SWEETER DRINK.

❧ COFFEE STOUT ❧

YIELD: 1 SERVING

Looking for a delicious beer-based cocktail? This one is hard to beat and it's really easy to make, too. Cheers!

INGREDIENTS

1 OUNCE (30 ML) BREWED, CHILLED LIVELY UP! COFFEE

1 OUNCE (30 ML) CHOCOLATE SIMPLE SYRUP (PAGE 125) OR REGULAR SIMPLE SYRUP (PAGE 118)

1 (14.9-OUNCE, OR 440 ML) CAN GUINNESS STOUT

WHIPPED CREAM, FOR GARNISH (OPTIONAL)

DIRECTIONS

In a 16-ounce (475 ml) glass, combine the coffee and simple syrup. Stir very well. Slowly pour in the stout, stirring as you pour. Garnish with whipped cream (if using).

TIP: AS AN ALTERNATIVE TO GUINNESS STOUT, USE A MICROBREWED MILK STOUT FOR THIS DRINK. MILK STOUT, OR SWEET STOUT, IS MADE WITH LACTOSE, A SUGAR FOUND IN MILK, TO ADD A HINT OF SWEETNESS.

A SELECTION OF SOUPS AND STEWS

(Talkin' Blues coffee)

Talkin' Blues is a single-origin coffee and it's a great choice for cooking. With a slight floral aroma and nicely balanced acidity, this full-bodied coffee is especially wonderful to use in soups and stews that simmer and bubble for a long time. Its flavor is enhanced rather than diluted in everything from a vegetarian chipotle chili or a steaming fish chowder enriched with heavy cream to a warming and restorative kidney bean soup that gets even better when served with freshly made dumplings.

Soup is one of those homey, filling, flavorful comfort foods that tastes even better the day after you make it, so many of the soups, stews, and chowders that follow are best made in advance. Whip up a big potful and eat it for several days! Soup making is flexible and forgiving. You don't have to be exacting to make soup, but you can be as creative as you like.

In this chapter, you'll find classics with a twist, like Coffee-Infused French Onion Soup (page 143) and Coffee Bean–Infused Pumpkin Soup (page 134) along with meal-in-a-bowl soups like Smoky Turkey and Black Bean Stew (page 140) and Coffee-Infused White Bean Stew (page 144). And for anyone who loves gumbo, the one on page 138, which contains andouille sausage as well as chicken, plus corn and okra (and coffee, of course), is a winner.

COFFEE-SPICED HEARTY VEGETARIAN CHIPOTLE CHILI

YIELD: 4 SERVINGS

This robustly flavored chili is not for the faint of heart. It's got big, assertive flavors—all perfectly mellowed by coffee. We like to eat this chili with cornbread, sour cream, sliced scallions, and thinly sliced jalapeño peppers.

INGREDIENTS

¼ CUP (60 ML) EXTRA-VIRGIN OLIVE OIL

2 TOMATOES, DICED

1 STALK CELERY, DICED

¼ CUP (40 G) DICED ONION (ABOUT ½ ONION)

2 CLOVES GARLIC, MINCED

1 BUNCH FRESH CILANTRO, STEMMED AND CHOPPED

2 TABLESPOONS CHILI POWDER, PLUS MORE AS NEEDED

2 TABLESPOONS GROUND CUMIN

2 CANNED CHIPOTLE CHILES IN ADOBO (ABOUT ¼ OF A 7-OUNCE, OR 195 G, CAN) CHOPPED

¼ CUP (65 G) TOMATO PASTE

3 TABLESPOONS (ABOUT 36 G) MARLEY COFFEE SPICE BLEND (PAGE 14)

1 CUP (256 G) CANNED WHITE BEANS, RINSED AND DRAINED

1 CUP (256 G) CANNED KIDNEY BEANS, RINSED AND DRAINED

1 CUP (262 G) CANNED NAVY BEANS, RINSED AND DRAINED

2 BAY LEAVES

2 CUPS (475 ML) VEGETABLE STOCK OR BROTH

1 CUP (25 G) FIRM TOFU, CRUMBLED

SALT AND FRESHLY GROUND BLACK PEPPER TO TASTE

AVOCADO SLICES, FOR GARNISH (OPTIONAL)

DIRECTIONS

Preheat a heavy 5-quart saucepan over medium heat for several minutes. When it is very hot, add the olive oil, tomatoes, celery, onion, garlic, cilantro, chili powder, cumin, chipotles, tomato paste, and Marley Coffee Spice Blend. Sauté for 4 minutes, stirring frequently, or until the vegetables soften.

Stir in the white beans, kidney beans, navy beans, bay leaves, and vegetable stock. Bring the mixture to a boil, reduce the heat to low, and simmer for 45 minutes, covered, or until the chili begins to thicken and some beans burst open.

Add the tofu in several additions, stirring carefully after each. Taste the chili and add additional chili powder, salt, and pepper as needed.

TIP: THE RECIPE CALLS FOR CANNED WHITE BEANS, KIDNEY BEANS, AND NAVY BEANS, BUT FEEL FREE TO USE ANY CANNED BEANS YOU PREFER.

❧ COFFEE BEAN–INFUSED PUMPKIN SOUP ❧

YIELD: 4 SERVINGS

Talkin' Blues, a pure-tasting coffee with a deep, earthy taste, nicely balances the flavor of the pumpkin here. If fresh pumpkins are not available, substitute two cans pure pumpkin purée (not pie filling). Add the purée to the pot with the other cooked and puréed vegetables. Serve as a first course, or any time you want a warming, comforting soup.

INGREDIENTS

2 TABLESPOONS (28 G) COCONUT OIL

2 MEDIUM-SIZE SUGAR PUMPKINS, QUARTERED, SEEDS REMOVED AND RESERVED

1 LARGE SWEET POTATO, PEELED AND QUARTERED

¼ YELLOW ONION, DICED

1 TABLESPOON MINCED FRESH GINGER

2 CLOVES GARLIC, CHOPPED

1 SPRIG FRESH THYME, CHOPPED

1 BAY LEAF

1½ CUPS (355 ML) VEGETABLE STOCK OR BROTH

¼ CUP (60 ML) BREWED TALKIN' BLUES COFFEE

½ CUP (120 ML) HEAVY CREAM

KOSHER SALT AND FRESHLY GROUND BLACK PEPPER TO TASTE

TOASTED PUMPKIN SEEDS, FOR GARNISH (SEE TIP)

DIRECTIONS

Preheat a large saucepan or a stockpot over medium heat until very hot. Add the coconut oil, pumpkins, sweet potato, and onion. Cook for 10 minutes, stirring occasionally, or until the vegetables begin to caramelize.

Stir in the ginger, garlic, thyme, bay leaf, vegetable stock, and coffee. Simmer for 35 minutes, or until the pumpkins and sweet potato are tender. Working in batches, purée the soup in a food processor, returning each batch to the saucepan once it is smooth. Reheat the mixture over medium-low heat.

Whisk in the heavy cream and season the soup with salt and pepper. Top each serving with toasted pumpkin seeds before serving.

TIP: TO TOAST THE PUMPKIN SEEDS, WASH THEM VERY WELL, DISCARD ANY STICKY MATERIAL CLINGING TO THEM, AND DRY THE SEEDS. TOSS WITH A LITTLE COCONUT OIL, SALT, AND PEPPER. ROAST IN A PREHEATED 375°F (190°C, OR GAS MARK 5) OVEN FOR 10 MINUTES, OR UNTIL CRISP.

I NAMED THIS COFFEE TALKIN'
BLUES AFTER MY FATHER'S
SONG. TALKIN' BLUES MEANS
LISTENING TO THE BLUES,
SITTING AROUND WITH A CUP
OF COFFEE, AND HAVING A
CONVERSATION. AND WHEN WE
LISTEN TO BLUES WE THINK OF
SLOW, LOW, AND CHILL. AND
WHAT DO WE DO WHEN WE ARE
CHILLING IN THE KITCHEN?
WE'RE MAKING SOUPS AND
STEWS. THEY COOK FOR A LONG
TIME—LONG AND SLOW. LONG,
SLOW COOKING IS WHAT YOU
NEED TO MAKE SURE THE SOUPS
AND STEWS TURN OUT THE BEST
THEY CAN BE.

❧ CHEF MAX'S GUMBO ❧

YIELD: 6 TO 8 SERVINGS

A rich sauce burnished by coffee sets this dish apart from other gumbos. This dish calls for a lot of ingredients, but it's not hard to make and it's a real crowd pleaser. Serve this hearty main course with rice and cornbread for a homey, filling meal.

INGREDIENTS

FOR GUMBO:

2 (3-POUND, OR 1.36 KG) CHICKENS, QUARTERED

1 BAY LEAF

1 SMALL YELLOW ONION, DICED

KOSHER SALT AND FRESHLY GROUND BLACK PEPPER TO TASTE

4 CUPS (946 ML) WATER

¼ CUP (60 ML) BREWED TALKIN' BLUES COFFEE

3 CLOVES GARLIC, MINCED

2 SPRIGS FRESH THYME, CHOPPED

2 ANDOUILLE SAUSAGES (ABOUT 2 POUNDS, OR 908 G), SLICED INTO ROUNDS

1 CUP (190 G) UNCOOKED RICE

3 TABLESPOONS (21 G) GUMBO FILÉ POWDER

2 TABLESPOONS (32 G) TOMATO PASTE

2 EARS FRESH CORN, HUSKED AND CUT INTO SIXTHS

10 WHOLE OKRA, CHOPPED

FOR ROUX:

½ POUND (2 STICKS, OR 225 G) UNSALTED BUTTER

1 CUP (112 G) ALL-PURPOSE FLOUR

DIRECTIONS

TO MAKE THE GUMBO:

In a large saucepan or a soup pot over medium-high heat, combine the chicken quarters, bay leaf, onion, salt, pepper, and water. Bring to a boil, reduce the heat to low, and simmer for 1½ hours, covered, or until the chicken is cooked and falling off the bone.

Remove the chicken from the pot to cool. Reserve the broth in the saucepan and let it simmer over low heat. When cool enough to handle, remove the chicken from the bones. Discard the skin and bones. Shred the chicken and set aside, covered.

To the reserved broth, stir in the coffee, garlic, thyme, sausage, rice, filé powder, and tomato paste. Bring to a boil, reduce the heat to low, and simmer for about 20 minutes. Add the corn, okra, and reserved chicken. Simmer for about 20 minutes more, or until the vegetables are tender.

TO MAKE THE ROUX:

In a small saucepan over low heat, melt the butter. Whisk in the flour and cook for about 10 minutes, stirring, or until it is a light brown color. Gradually whisk the roux into the soup. Continue to whisk until it is all incorporated and the liquid is thick and smooth. Taste the soup and add additional salt and pepper, if desired.

> **NOTE:** Produced from the leaves of the sassafras tree, filé (pronounced FEE-lay) powder is typically added as a thickener and flavor agent to soups and gumbos. You can find gumbo filé powder online or in specialty food stores.

❧ SMOKY TURKEY AND BLACK BEAN STEW ❧

YIELD: 4 TO 6 SERVINGS

A delicious meal in a pot is flavored with smoked turkey, cumin, and fresh thyme, plus an infusion of brewed coffee for the extra flavor spark.

INGREDIENTS

1 WHOLE SMOKED TURKEY WING

6 CUPS (1.43 L) WATER

4 (15.5-OUNCE, OR 439 G) CANS BLACK BEANS, RINSED AND DRAINED

3 BAY LEAVES

3 CLOVES GARLIC, DICED

1 STALK CELERY, DICED

3 TABLESPOONS CHOPPED FRESH THYME LEAVES

½ YELLOW ONION, DICED

2 TOMATOES, DICED

3 TABLESPOONS (21 G) GROUND CUMIN

½ CUP (120 ML) BREWED, COOLED TALKIN' BLUES COFFEE

½ RED BELL PEPPER, CORED, SEEDED, AND DICED

½ GREEN BELL PEPPER, CORED, SEEDED, AND DICED

2 SCALLIONS (WHITE AND LIGHT GREEN PARTS), CHOPPED, FOR GARNISH

DIRECTIONS

In a large stockpot over medium-high heat, combine the turkey wing and water. Bring to a boil, reduce the heat to low, and simmer the turkey for 1 hour, or until it is tender and falling off the bone. Remove the turkey from the pot, but don't drain the water. When the turkey is cool enough to handle, remove the meat from the bone. Shred the meat. Return it to the pot.

Stir in the black beans, bay leaves, garlic, celery, thyme, onion, tomatoes, cumin, and coffee. Simmer for 45 minutes. Add the diced red and green bell peppers and simmer for 10 minutes more. Serve garnished with the scallions.

TIP: IF YOU LIKE, TOP EACH BOWLFUL WITH SOUR CREAM AND SERVE WITH A SIDE OF CORNBREAD.

❖ COFFEE-INFUSED FISH CHOWDER ❖

YIELD: 8 SERVINGS

Enriched with cream and tempered by a little coffee, this delicious chowder smells delicious as it simmers and it will warm you on any cold day.

INGREDIENTS

FOR CHOWDER:

1 CUP (218 G) COCONUT OIL

3 YUKON GOLD POTATOES, PEELED AND DICED

3 STALKS CELERY, DICED

2 CARROTS, PEELED AND DICED

1 SMALL YELLOW ONION, DICED

2 CLOVES GARLIC, MINCED

2 SPRIGS FRESH THYME, STEMMED AND CHOPPED

KOSHER SALT AND FRESHLY GROUND BLACK PEPPER TO TASTE

1 POUND (454 G) GROUPER FILLETS

3 CUPS (705 ML) FISH STOCK OR BROTH, OR VEGETABLE STOCK OR BROTH

2 CUPS (475 ML) HEAVY CREAM

¼ CUP (60 ML) BREWED, COOLED TALKIN' BLUES COFFEE

FOR ROUX:

½ POUND (2 STICKS, OR 225 G) UNSALTED BUTTER

½ CUP (56 G) ALL-PURPOSE FLOUR

DIRECTIONS

TO MAKE THE CHOWDER:

Preheat a large stockpot over medium heat for 2 minutes, or until very hot. Add the coconut oil, potatoes, celery, carrots, onion, garlic, and thyme. Season with salt and pepper. Reduce the heat to low and cook for 10 minutes, stirring occasionally, or until the vegetables are fork-tender.

Add the grouper and continue to cook for 3 more minutes. Pour in the fish stock, bring to a boil, and reduce the heat to low. Simmer for 15 minutes. Stir in the heavy cream and coffee. Simmer for 10 minutes more, or until very hot.

TO MAKE THE ROUX:

In a small heavy saucepan over low heat, melt the butter. Whisk in the flour and cook for 3 to 5 minutes, stirring until the mixture is golden and the butter is well incorporated into the flour.

Add the roux to the soup in several parts, whisking very well after each addition. Once the soup is smooth and thick, reduce the heat to low and simmer for about 10 minutes, or until very hot. Taste and add additional salt and pepper, if desired.

TIP: THIS SOUP IS DELICIOUS SERVED IN WIDE BOWLS AND TOPPED WITH CORN BREAD CROUTONS OR OYSTER CRACKERS.

COFFEE SPICE BLEND–INFUSED
❖ KIDNEY BEAN SOUP WITH DUMPLINGS ❖

YIELD: 6 TO 8 SERVINGS

A meal in itself, this thick, restorative soup has an abundant supply of vegetables and a wonderful, rich flavor from the coffee. Dumplings add body to this old-fashioned potage, which will leave your kitchen smelling homey and delicious. Max's mother added pigtails or salt pork to this soup, which she would make on a Sunday night and eat all week. You could also put in some smoked turkey.

INGREDIENTS

FOR SOUP:

2 POUNDS (908 G) DRIED KIDNEY BEANS

3 BAY LEAVES, DIVIDED

½ CUP (109 G) COCONUT OIL

4 SCALLIONS (WHITE AND LIGHT GREEN PARTS), CHOPPED, DIVIDED

1 YELLOW ONION, DICED

2 CLOVES GARLIC, MINCED

1 TABLESPOON CHOPPED FRESH GINGER

1 TABLESPOON MARLEY COFFEE SPICE BLEND (PAGE 14)

2 SPRIGS FRESH THYME, CHOPPED

3 CUPS (705 ML) VEGETABLE STOCK OR BROTH

¼ CUP (60 ML) BREWED TALKIN' BLUES COFFEE

FOR DUMPLINGS:

1 CUP (112 G) ALL-PURPOSE FLOUR, PLUS MORE FOR DUSTING YOUR HANDS

½ CUP (120 ML) WATER

1 CUP (235 ML) COCONUT MILK

KOSHER SALT AND FRESHLY GROUND BLACK PEPPER TO TASTE

DIRECTIONS

TO MAKE THE SOUP:

In a large, heavy saucepan over medium-high heat, combine the kidney beans, 2 bay leaves, and enough water to cover. Cover, bring to a boil, and reduce the heat to medium-low. Cook the beans for about 2 hours, covered, stirring occasionally, or until fork-tender. Drain the beans and set them aside, covered.

Return the pan to the heat and add the coconut oil, half of the scallions, the onion, garlic, ginger, remaining bay leaf, Marley Coffee Spice Blend, and thyme. Sauté for about 5 minutes, or until the vegetables begin to soften.

Return the beans to the pan and reduce the heat to low. Stir in the vegetable stock and coffee. Cook for about 25 minutes, stirring frequently.

TO MAKE THE DUMPLINGS:

Place the flour in a small bowl and slowly add the water, mixing with your fingers until a soft dough forms. Flour your hands and roll the dough into finger-shaped dumplings, ½ inch to 1 inch (1 to 2.5 cm) each. Carefully transfer the dumplings to the saucepan and let them simmer in the soup for about 15 minutes, or until cooked through.

Whisk in the coconut milk and simmer for 10 minutes more, or until very hot. Season with salt and pepper. Serve the soup garnished with the remaining scallions.

TIP: IF YOU HAVE ANY LEFTOVERS, THIS SOUP FREEZES WELL.

❧ COFFEE-INFUSED FRENCH ONION SOUP ❧

YIELD: 5 SERVINGS

Coffee lends body to this delicious classic, and the provolone, Swiss, and Parmesan cheeses contribute to the deliciousness.

INGREDIENTS

1 LOAF CHALLAH BREAD, SLICED ¼ INCH (6 MM) THICK

½ POUND (2 STICKS, OR 225 G) UNSALTED BUTTER

3 CLOVES GARLIC, MINCED

6 YELLOW ONIONS, JULIENNED

2 BAY LEAVES

¼ CUP (80 G) BEEF BASE PLUS ¾ CUP (175 ML) WATER, OR 1 CUP (235 ML) BEEF STOCK

½ CUP (120 ML) DRY SHERRY

¼ CUP (60 ML) BREWED TALKIN' BLUES COFFEE

¼ CUP (60 ML) BRANDY

¼ CUP (60 ML) WORCESTERSHIRE SAUCE

KOSHER SALT AND FRESHLY GROUND BLACK PEPPER TO TASTE

¼ POUND (55 G) PROVOLONE CHEESE, SLICED

¼ POUND (55 G) SWISS CHEESE, SLICED

¼ CUP (20 G) SHAVED PARMESAN CHEESE

DIRECTIONS

Preheat the oven to 400°F (200°C, or gas mark 6). Place the challah slices on a parchment paper–lined baking sheet. Bake for about 10 minutes, or until crisp.

Preheat a large stockpot or saucepan over medium heat for 2 minutes, or until very hot. Add the butter to melt. Stir in the garlic, onions, and bay leaves. Reduce the heat to low and cook for about 10 minutes, stirring, or until the onions are brown and appear to be caramelized.

Stir in the beef base, sherry, coffee, brandy, and Worcestershire sauce. Season with salt and pepper. Bring to a boil, reduce the heat to low, and simmer for about 45 minutes.

Preheat the broiler.

Ladle the soup into 5 large heatproof soup bowls. Top each with some toasted challah, slices of provolone and Swiss, and Parmesan shavings. Place the soup bowls on a flameproof baking sheet. Broil for about 1½ minutes, or until the cheese melts.

NOTE: When selecting onions at the store, choose those that are heavy for their size and that have no soft spots. They should have papery, dry skins and no signs of moistness. Onions can be kept in a cool, dry place for as long as 2 months—depending on their condition when you bought them.

❧ COFFEE-INFUSED WHITE BEAN STEW ❧

YIELD: 8 SERVINGS

With plenty of spices and a splash of coffee, this stew tastes fresh and smells wonderful. If you use vegetable stock rather than chicken stock, you can serve this savory dish to anyone in your squad who doesn't eat meat.

INGREDIENTS

¼ CUP (55 G) COCONUT OIL

2 STALKS CELERY, DICED

2 RED BELL PEPPERS, CORED, SEEDED, AND CHOPPED

1 CARROT, DICED

½ YELLOW ONION, DICED

½ LEEK, CLEANED THOROUGHLY AND DICED

¼ BUNCH KALE, TRIMMED AND CHOPPED

3 CLOVES GARLIC, CHOPPED

2 BAY LEAVES

2 TABLESPOONS CHOPPED FRESH THYME LEAVES

¼ CUP (60 ML) BREWED TALKIN' BLUES COFFEE

3 TABLESPOONS (20 G) TURMERIC

1 TABLESPOON GROUND CUMIN

3 (16-OUNCE, OR 455 G) CANS WHITE BEANS, RINSED AND DRAINED

2 CUPS (475 ML) VEGETABLE STOCK OR BROTH, OR CHICKEN STOCK OR BROTH

RADISH SLICES AND LIME WEDGES, FOR GARNISH

DIRECTIONS

In a large stockpot over medium heat, heat the coconut oil until very hot. Add the celery, red bell peppers, carrot, onion, leek, kale, garlic, bay leaves, and thyme. Reduce the heat to medium-low and cook for about 5 minutes, stirring occasionally, or until the vegetables begin to soften.

Stir in the coffee, turmeric, cumin, white beans, and vegetable stock. Increase the heat to medium and bring to a boil. Reduce the heat to low and simmer for about 1 hour, stirring occasionally. Serve garnished with radish slices and lime wedges.

TIP: USE WHATEVER VARIETY OF WHITE BEANS YOU LIKE FOR THIS STEW. FEEL FREE TO MAKE THE STEW A DAY OR TWO AHEAD OF TIME AND REHEAT SLOWLY, STIRRING OFTEN.

ROBUSTLY FLAVORED MEAT AND SEAFOOD

(Buffalo Soldier coffee)

Buffalo Soldier coffee, or another rich, assertive coffee, is an ideal choice to pair with hearty, flavorful roasts and steaks, as well as salmon, duck, and lamb. Where it might be too much for a light salad or delicate vegetable, a good, bold coffee is just perfect for a marinade, glaze, or sauce for a rich cut of meat or seafood. Salmon, for instance, becomes even better when sauced with a coffee glaze mellowed by maple syrup and enlivened with fresh ginger and garlic. Rich, gamey duck breast shines when marinated in a coffee-based brine that contains soy sauce, star anise, and freshly squeezed orange juice. Grouper is marinated in a mixture that contains ginger and finely ground coffee beans before cooking, which imparts delicious flavor to this fish. And meatballs are promoted from the ordinary to the extraordinary when flavored with Marley Coffee Spice Blend and curry powder and finished with a coffee and teriyaki glaze.

Feel free to experiment and be creative with coffee when cooking meat, poultry, and fish. Consider adding a drizzle to marinades and sauces. You will be surprised at how the coffee brings out the best in beef, pork, lamb, chicken, and seafood!

TERIYAKI SALMON

YIELD: 6 SERVINGS

The coffee in this sauce enriches the teriyaki and brings out the flavor of the salmon. The grilled lemon garnish adds extra zip.

INGREDIENTS

¼ CUP (55 G) COCONUT OIL

6 (8-OUNCE, OR 225 G) SKIN-ON SALMON FILLETS

1 POUND (454 G) TOMATOES OF YOUR CHOICE, CUT INTO CHUNKS

½ RED BELL PEPPER, CORED, SEEDED, AND JULIENNED

¼ YELLOW ONION, DICED

2 CLOVES GARLIC, CHOPPED

½ CUP (120 ML) TERIYAKI SAUCE

¼ CUP (60 ML) BREWED, COOLED BUFFALO SOLDIER COFFEE

1 TEASPOON CORNSTARCH

¼ BUNCH FRESH CILANTRO, STEMMED AND CHOPPED, OR LEFT IN SPRIGS FOR GARNISH

GRILLED LEMONS, FOR GARNISH (SEE TIP)

KOSHER SALT AND FRESHLY GROUND BLACK PEPPER TO TASTE

DIRECTIONS

Preheat a large skillet or sauté pan over medium heat until very hot. Add the coconut oil. When it sizzles, add the salmon, skin-side down. Sear for about 3 minutes, or until the skin is crisp. With a large spatula, flip the salmon and cook it on the other side for about 3 minutes. Add the tomatoes, red bell pepper, onion, and garlic. Cook for about 3 minutes.

Remove the salmon from the pan and pour in the teriyaki sauce and coffee. Bring the mixture to a rolling boil over medium heat; reduce the heat to low and whisk in the cornstarch. Cook the sauce, stirring, until it thickens and the cornstarch dissolves. Return the salmon to the pan and cook it for another 3 minutes, or until the fish flakes easily with a fork.

To plate, drizzle or pour some sauce on a plate, arrange a portion of salmon on top, and garnish with cilantro and grilled lemon. Season with salt and pepper.

TIP: TO GRILL LEMONS, HALVE THEM AND PLACE THEM, CUT-SIDES DOWN, ON A GRILL FOR ABOUT 2 MINUTES OVER MEDIUM-HIGH HEAT, OR UNTIL THEY SOFTEN AND DEVELOP GRILL MARKS.

CEDAR PLANK SALMON WITH
❖ COFFEE, MAPLE, AND LEMON GLAZE ❖

YIELD: 6 SERVINGS

A smooth coffee with dark chocolate undertones is the basis for a glaze for this lush salmon dish, which would be delicious with roasted new potatoes and a big green salad. You'll need a presoaked cedar plank to cook the salmon, but these are easy to find in any store that sells grills.

INGREDIENTS

½ CUP (120 ML) MAPLE SYRUP

⅓ CUP (78 ML) LOW-SODIUM SOY SAUCE

¼ CUP (60 ML) FRESHLY SQUEEZED LEMON JUICE

¼ CUP (60 ML) BREWED BUFFALO SOLDIER COFFEE

1 TABLESPOON CHOPPED FRESH GINGER

1 TABLESPOON CHOPPED FRESH GARLIC

1 BUNCH SCALLIONS (WHITE AND LIGHT GREEN PARTS), ENDS TRIMMED

1 (4-POUND, OR 1.8 KG) SKIN-ON SALMON FILLET

DIRECTIONS

In a medium-size saucepan over medium heat, stir together the maple syrup, soy sauce, lemon juice, coffee, ginger, and garlic. Bring to a boil; reduce the heat to low, and cook the glaze for 6 to 8 minutes, stirring occasionally, or until reduced by half.

Preheat a gas or charcoal grill to medium for about 10 minutes.

On a presoaked cedar plank, arrange the scallions. Place the salmon on top. Place the plank on the grill, close the grill lid, and cook for 10 minutes. Baste the salmon with the glaze, and continue to baste about every 5 minutes. Grill for about 15 minutes more, or until the fish reaches 145°F (62.7°C) on an instant-read thermometer. Transfer the salmon from the cedar plank to a serving platter. Baste again with some of the remaining glaze and serve.

GRILLED TURKEY CHOPS
❧ WITH MANGO-CRANBERRY CHUTNEY ❧

YIELD: 4 SERVINGS

Elevate the traditional combination of turkey and cranberries by adding some Marley Coffee Spice Blend (page 14), along with fresh mango, lime juice, and thyme. You will need to ask your butcher for turkey chops, which resemble pork chops. If they are unavailable, substitute turkey cutlets. Grilling the turkey gives it a delectable appearance and taste.

INGREDIENTS

1½ POUNDS (680 G) TURKEY CHOPS OR TURKEY CUTLETS

2 TABLESPOONS (30 ML) EXTRA-VIRGIN OLIVE OIL

1 TABLESPOON MARLEY COFFEE SPICE BLEND (PAGE 14)

2 SPRIGS FRESH SAGE, CHOPPED

2 CLOVES GARLIC, MINCED

2 RIPE MANGOS, PEELED, PITTED, AND DICED

1 CUP (100 G) FRESH CRANBERRIES

¼ CUP (50 G) SUGAR

3 SPRIGS FRESH THYME, STEMMED AND CHOPPED

2 TABLESPOONS (30 ML) FRESHLY SQUEEZED LIME JUICE

NOTE: Not sure how to choose a mango? Look for larger ones because they have a higher fruit-to-seed ratio, and choose those that have a yellow skin lightly blushed with red. To ripen hard mangos, place them in a paper bag and set aside at room temperature for a day or two.

DIRECTIONS

Arrange the turkey chops in a large, shallow baking pan.

In a medium-size bowl, whisk the olive oil, Marley Coffee Spice Blend, sage, and garlic. Pour this marinade over the turkey. Cover and set aside for at least 35 minutes. Or you can marinate the meat, covered and refrigerated, overnight.

Preheat a charcoal grill to medium or place a grill pan over medium heat.

• If using a grill, once the coals are gray place the chops, skin-side up, on the grill. Grill for 10 minutes, flip, and grill for about 10 minutes more, or until they are thoroughly cooked. Keep an eye on the grill to make sure it's not too hot.

• If using a grill pan, cook the chops for 10 minutes, flip, and cook until done.

You will know your chops are done when they are firm to the touch and have reached an internal temperature of 165°F (74°C), measured with a meat thermometer. Some chops are thinner than others and will cook more quickly.

Meanwhile, in a medium-size saucepan over medium heat, stir together the mangos, cranberries, sugar, thyme, and lime juice. Bring to a simmer and cook for 5 minutes, stirring constantly, or until the fruit softens and the sugar dissolves. Serve the chutney with the chops.

COFFEE-INFUSED PAELLA

YIELD: 6 TO 8 SERVINGS

Coffee enriches this classic paella, teasing out the flavors in this very special dish. Our version, which contains an abundance of fresh herbs, is lively, colorful, and perfect to serve at a party.

INGREDIENTS

2 (3-POUND, OR 1.36 KG) CHICKENS, QUARTERED

2 TABLESPOONS (ABOUT 24 G) MARLEY COFFEE SPICE BLEND (PAGE 14)

2 LEMONS, DIVIDED

1 BUNCH FRESH CILANTRO, STEMMED AND CHOPPED, DIVIDED

1 CUP (235 ML) LIGHT EXTRA-VIRGIN OLIVE OIL

4 CUPS (740 G) PAELLA RICE OR REGULAR LONG-GRAIN RICE

4 CLOVES GARLIC, MINCED

1 YELLOW ONION, DICED

1 RED BELL PEPPER, CORED, SEEDED, AND CHOPPED

1 YELLOW BELL PEPPER, CORED, SEEDED, AND CHOPPED

1 GREEN BELL PEPPER, CORED, SEEDED, AND CHOPPED

2 TOMATOES, CHOPPED

1 BUNCH FRESH THYME, STEMMED AND CHOPPED

PINCH SAFFRON THREADS

2 QUARTS (1.89 L) CHICKEN STOCK OR BROTH

1 CUP (235 ML) DRY WHITE WINE

1 CUP (235 ML) BREWED, COOLED BUFFALO SOLDIER COFFEE

1 POUND (454 G) LARGE SHRIMP, SHELLED AND DEVEINED

1 POUND (454 G) ANDOUILLE SAUSAGE, CUT INTO BITE-SIZE PIECES

KOSHER SALT AND FRESHLY GROUND BLACK PEPPER TO TASTE

DIRECTIONS

In a large bowl, combine the chicken, Marley Coffee Spice Blend, juice of 1 lemon, and half of the cilantro. Toss until the chicken is fully coated.

In a large paella pan, skillet, or sauté pan over medium heat, heat the olive oil for 2 minutes. Add the chicken and sear it for about 4 minutes per side, or until golden brown. You may have to do this in batches. Stir in the rice, garlic, onion, red, yellow, and green

bell peppers, tomatoes, and thyme. Add the saffron, chicken stock, white wine, coffee, shrimp, and andouille sausage. Cover the pan and simmer for 20 minutes, or until the rice is tender and the liquid is completely absorbed.

Spoon the paella into a large serving dish. Slice the remaining lemon and garnish the paella with lemon slices and the remaining cilantro. Season with salt and pepper.

NOTE: Saffron, which is a very costly spice, is the yellow-orange stigmas from a diminutive purple crocus. Pungent and aromatic, it is used both to tint and flavor food, and is essential to paella. Store saffron in an airtight container in a dark, cool place for no longer than six months.

ASIAN DUCK BREAST MARINATED ❖ IN COFFEE BRINE ❖

YIELD: 4 SERVINGS

Duck can be gamey, but it has a light flavor that needs something to bolster it. In this dish, the coffee brine takes away some of the gaminess while adding a deep, complex flavor. The pickling spice, sweet and earthy with some herbal tones, is a nice addition to the brine.

INGREDIENTS

FOR BRINE:

4 CUPS (946 ML) BREWED BUFFALO SOLDIER COFFEE

½ CUP (50 G) PICKLING SPICE

½ CUP (120 G) FIRMLY PACKED LIGHT BROWN SUGAR

1 (1-INCH, OR 2.5 CM) PIECE FRESH GINGER, UNPEELED, SLICED

¼ CUP (60 ML) EXTRA-VIRGIN OLIVE OIL

¼ CUP (60 ML) LOW-SODIUM SOY SAUCE

2 BAY LEAVES

1 ORANGE, HALVED

2 STAR ANISE

SALT AND FRESHLY GROUND BLACK PEPPER TO TASTE

FOR DUCK:

4 (6- TO 8-OUNCE, OR 170 TO 225 G) BONELESS DUCK BREASTS

¼ CUP (60 ML) EXTRA-VIRGIN OLIVE OIL

DIRECTIONS

TO MAKE THE BRINE:

In a large glass bowl, combine the coffee, pickling spice, brown sugar, ginger, olive oil, soy sauce, and bay leaves. Squeeze the orange juice into the bowl and add the rinds. Vigorously stir in the star anise, salt, and pepper to mix well.

TO MAKE THE DUCK:

Place the duck breasts in the brine, cover with plastic wrap, and refrigerate for at least 1½ hours or, preferably, overnight.

Preheat the oven to 400°F (200°C, or gas mark 6). Remove the duck breasts from the brine and pat them dry with paper towels. Discard the brine.

Preheat a large skillet or sauté pan over medium heat. When the pan is very hot, add the olive oil. After about 30 seconds, add the duck, fat-side down. Sauté for 5 to 6 minutes, or until all the fat is rendered. The skin will become crispy and turn a nice golden, caramelized color. With large tongs, flip the duck breasts and cook for 1 to 2 minutes more. Transfer the duck to a baking sheet.

Place the duck in the oven and roast for about 6 minutes, or until medium-rare. When ready, the inside of the duck should be a nice rosy pink. Remove from the oven and let rest for 4 to 5 minutes. Slice the duck ¼ inch (6 mm) thick.

TIP: THIS DISH IS DELICIOUS SERVED WITH GRILLED PEACHES WITH COFFEE (PAGE 94).

HONEY AND COFFEE
❧ CHICKEN WINGS ❧

YIELD: 4 TO 6 SERVINGS AS AN APPETIZER

A splash of richly flavored coffee cuts the honey's sweetness in this delightful marinade, which is used here on chicken wings destined for the grill. Make plenty of these tasty wings, which always seem to be the first of the appetizers to disappear.

INGREDIENTS

1 CUP (340 G) HONEY

¼ POUND (1 STICK, OR 113 G) UNSALTED BUTTER

¼ CUP (60 ML) BREWED BUFFALO SOLDIER COFFEE

2 TABLESPOONS (20 G) MINCED GARLIC (ABOUT 6 LARGE CLOVES)

2 TABLESPOONS (ABOUT 24 G) MARLEY COFFEE SPICE BLEND (PAGE 14)

1 TABLESPOON CHOPPED FRESH THYME LEAVES

1 TABLESPOON (15 ML) EXTRA-VIRGIN OLIVE OIL

1 TABLESPOON CHILI POWDER

1 TABLESPOON GROUND CUMIN

KOSHER SALT AND FRESHLY GROUND BLACK PEPPER TO TASTE

2 POUNDS (908 G) CHICKEN WINGS, CUT AT THE JOINT TO REMOVE THE TIPS

DIRECTIONS

In a medium-size saucepan over medium heat, whisk the honey, butter, coffee, garlic, Marley Coffee Spice Blend, thyme, olive oil, chili powder, cumin, salt, and pepper. Whisking constantly, bring to a boil. Reduce the heat to low and simmer for about 3 minutes. Remove from the heat and let cool.

Measure ½ cup (120 ml) marinade and set aside. Place the wings in a large resealable plastic bag and pour in the remaining marinade. Seal the bag and refrigerate the wings to marinate for 1 hour, or overnight.

Preheat a grill to medium. Place the wings on the grill and grill for about 15 minutes per side, turning occasionally. While the wings are cooking, brush them occasionally with the reserved ½ cup (120 ml) marinade. When the wings reach an internal temperature of 165°F (74°C) on an instant-read thermometer, remove them from the grill and place on a serving platter.

TIP: WATCH THESE WINGS CAREFULLY AND REMOVE THEM PROMPTLY FROM THE GRILL TO AVOID HAVING THEM BECOME CHARRED.

COFFEE-BRAISED ASIAN LAMB RIBS

YIELD: 4 SERVINGS

Lamb can really stand up to bold flavors, so a coffee like Buffalo Soldier, with its overtones of berries and chocolate, is perfect in this dish starring lamb ribs. While you can sometimes find lamb ribs in a supermarket, you may need to order them from your butcher.

INGREDIENTS

3 POUNDS (1.36 KG) LAMB RIBS

3 CLOVES GARLIC, MINCED

3 TABLESPOONS CHOPPED FRESH ROSEMARY

1 CUP (250 G) HOISIN SAUCE

1 (10-OUNCE, OR 285 ML) BOTTLE SAKE BEER

2 CARROTS, ROUGHLY CHOPPED

1 YELLOW ONION, ROUGHLY CHOPPED

1 CUP (235 ML) BEEF STOCK OR BROTH

1 CUP (235 ML) BREWED, COOLED BUFFALO SOLDIER COFFEE, OR A SIMILAR VARIETY

¼ CUP (25 G) SLICED SCALLIONS

FRIED (OR BAKED) WONTON CRISPS

2 TABLESPOONS (ABOUT 24 G) MARLEY COFFEE SPICE BLEND (PAGE 14)

DIRECTIONS

Preheat the oven to 375°F (190°C, or gas mark 5). In a large bowl, combine the lamb, garlic, rosemary, hoisin, and sake beer. Toss well to coat the ribs thoroughly with this marinade. Let the ribs marinate for 45 minutes in the refrigerator.

In the bottom of a very large rimmed baking pan, place the carrots and onion. This is your mirepoix (see note). Arrange the ribs on top of the vegetables and pour the marinade over the ribs. Pour the beef stock over the ribs and cover them with parchment paper. Wrap with a layer of aluminum foil. Bake for 1½ hours, or until fork-tender.

Transfer the ribs to a serving platter. Carefully pour the reduced liquid from the pan into a saucepan and place it over high heat. Reserve the mirepoix vegetables. Bring the liquid to a boil, reduce the heat to low, and simmer for 1 to 2 minutes. Glaze the ribs with liquid. Garnish with the scallions, wonton crisps, and Marley Coffee Spice Blend and serve with the reserved vegetables.

NOTE: A traditional mirepoix is a blend of diced carrots, celery, onion, and various herbs, usually cooked in butter. It adds flavor to whatever you cook with it.

CURRY MEATBALLS WITH ROASTED GARLIC,
❧ COFFEE, AND TERIYAKI GLAZE ❧

YIELD: 4 SERVINGS

These succulent meatballs, which get a burst of flavor from the Marley Coffee Spice Blend (page 14), are paired with a delicious teriyaki-based glaze that is enhanced with coffee. Make these ahead and freeze the meatballs, if you like, but don't freeze the glaze.

INGREDIENTS

FOR MEATBALLS:

2 POUNDS (908 G) GROUND CHICKEN

3 TABLESPOONS (19 G) CURRY POWDER

1 CLOVE GARLIC, MINCED

¼ BUNCH FRESH CILANTRO, STEMMED AND CHOPPED, DIVIDED

2 EGGS, LIGHTLY BEATEN

1 TABLESPOON MARLEY COFFEE SPICE BLEND (PAGE 14)

KOSHER SALT AND FRESHLY GROUND BLACK PEPPER TO TASTE

FOR GLAZE:

¼ CUP (60 ML) BREWED BUFFALO SOLDIER COFFEE

½ CUP (120 ML) TERIYAKI SAUCE

3 CLOVES ROASTED GARLIC (SEE TIP)

½ CUP (75 G) CHERRY TOMATOES

DIRECTIONS

TO MAKE THE MEATBALLS:

In a large bowl, mix the chicken, curry powder, garlic, most of the cilantro (reserve 3 tablespoons for garnish), the eggs, and Marley Coffee Spice Blend. Season with salt and pepper. Form the mixture into about 15 (2-inch, or 5 cm) meatballs.

Preheat a gas or electric grill to medium. Arrange the meatballs on the grill and grill for about 5 minutes per side. When thoroughly cooked, remove the meatballs from the grill and keep warm.

MEANWHILE, TO MAKE THE GLAZE:

In a medium-size saucepan over high heat, whisk the coffee, teriyaki sauce, roasted garlic, and cherry tomatoes. Whisking constantly, bring to a boil. Reduce the heat to low and simmer the glaze for 4 to 6 minutes, or until it starts to thicken.

Combine the cooked meatballs with the glaze and transfer to a serving bowl. Garnish with the reserved cilantro.

TIP: TO PREPARE ROASTED GARLIC, SPRINKLE THE GARLIC CLOVES WITH SALT AND PEPPER, RUB THEM WITH EXTRA-VIRGIN OLIVE OIL, AND WRAP THEM IN ALUMINUM FOIL. BAKE IN A PREHEATED 350°F (180°C, OR GAS MARK 4) OVEN FOR ABOUT 30 MINUTES, OR UNTIL VERY SOFT. LET COOL, SQUEEZE THE GARLIC PULP OUT OF THE SKINS, AND COMBINE IT WITH THE INGREDIENTS FOR THE GLAZE.

TIP: THESE MEATBALLS MAY ALSO BE BAKED IN A PREHEATED 350°F (180°C, OR GAS MARK 4) OVEN FOR ABOUT 25 MINUTES, OR UNTIL DONE.

I KNEW IF I WANTED TO LEARN ABOUT
COFFEE, I HAD TO LEARN ABOUT THE
ORIGINS OF COFFEE AND THE CULTURE
OF COFFEE. I NEEDED TO GO INTO THE
COFFEE COMMUNITY. THERE IS A SOCIAL
SIDE TO COFFEE. WHEN I BOUGHT
LAND IN JAMAICA, I SET OUT TO LEARN
EVERYTHING I COULD ABOUT COFFEE.
I LEARNED THAT COFFEE NEEDS SHADE
TREES AND THAT TOO MUCH SUN CAN
BURN THE COFFEE. I LEARNED THAT
YOU HAVE TO POLISH THE BEANS, AND
GRADE THEM, AND SORT THEM BY HAND.
IT'S IMPORTANT THAT YOU KNOW WHERE
THE COFFEE COMES FROM, AND THAT
YOU UNDERSTAND THE TASTE PROFILE
OF EACH TYPE OF COFFEE.

CARAMELIZED BRUSSELS SPROUTS WITH HONEY ALMONDS, ❖ SHALLOTS, AND TURKEY BACON ❖

YIELD: 4 TO 6 SERVINGS

For this recipe, you'll blanch the Brussels sprouts, which involves cooking them briefly in boiling water and "shocking" them with ice-cold water. The process keeps them crisp and maintains their green color. Serve this unusually good vegetable dish (with lots of flavor from the turkey bacon) with grilled meats or fish.

INGREDIENTS

1 POUND (454 G) BRUSSELS SPROUTS

1 POUND (454 G) TURKEY BACON, DICED

3 TABLESPOONS (42 G) UNSALTED BUTTER

4 SHALLOTS, SLICED THIN

3 OUNCES (85 G) HONEY-FLAVORED ALMONDS

2 TABLESPOONS (ABOUT 24 G) MARLEY COFFEE SPICE BLEND (PAGE 14)

KOSHER SALT AND FRESHLY GROUND BLACK PEPPER TO TASTE

DIRECTIONS

In a large stockpot of boiling salted water over medium heat, blanch the Brussels sprouts for 2 minutes. Drain them into a colander and immediately transfer to a large bowl of ice water. After about 1 minute, drain them again. Trim and halve the Brussels sprouts.

Preheat a large skillet or sauté pan over high heat for 1 to 2 minutes, or until very hot. Add the diced turkey bacon and cook until crisp. Transfer the turkey bacon to a plate and set aside. Pour the fat into a small heatproof container and set aside.

In the same pan over medium heat, heat 3 tablespoons (45 ml) reserved bacon fat and the butter until the butter begins to foam. Add the Brussels sprouts to the pan, cut-side down. Do not crowd the pan—you may need to do this in batches. Allow the Brussels sprouts to brown well or caramelize on the cut side for 3 to 4 minutes before turning. Add the shallots and cook for about 2 minutes. Stir in the reserved turkey bacon, almonds, and Marley Coffee Spice Blend. Season with salt and pepper.

TIP: YOU CAN PREPARE THIS DISH UP TO 1 HOUR BEFORE YOU PLAN TO SERVE IT. WARM ON THE STOVETOP BEFORE SERVING.

ROBUSTLY FLAVORED MEAT AND SEAFOOD

MISO- AND COFFEE-BROILED GROUPER

YIELD: 4 SERVINGS

Allow a few hours for the grouper to marinate in this coffee-fueled marinade. It's delicious served with rice and a big green salad.

INGREDIENTS

4 (8-OUNCE, OR 225 G) GROUPER FILLETS

KOSHER SALT AND FRESHLY GROUND BLACK PEPPER TO TASTE

½ CUP (125 G) MISO PASTE

2 TABLESPOONS FINELY GROUND BUFFALO SOLDIER COFFEE BEANS

2 TABLESPOONS MINCED FRESH GINGER

2 CLOVES GARLIC, MINCED

½ POUND (2 STICKS, OR 225 G) UNSALTED BUTTER, DIVIDED

¼ CUP (60 ML) MIRIN

1 TEASPOON PACKED LIGHT BROWN SUGAR

1 BUNCH ASPARAGUS, TRIMMED

1 CUP (70 G) SLICED SHIITAKE MUSHROOMS

2 TABLESPOONS (ABOUT 24 G) MARLEY COFFEE SPICE BLEND (PAGE 14)

DIRECTIONS

On a large rimmed baking pan, arrange the grouper fillets in a single layer. Sprinkle with salt and pepper.

In a medium-size bowl, whisk the miso paste, coffee, ginger, and garlic. Spoon this over the grouper, turning the fillets to coat both sides. Cover the baking pan and marinate the grouper, refrigerated, for a few hours or overnight. Bring to room temperature before broiling.

Preheat the broiler to high. Transfer the grouper to a rimmed baking sheet. Cut 1 stick of butter into small pieces and place them on top of the grouper. Broil for 15 minutes, or until golden brown and completely cooked. Remove the fish from the broiler and pour any accumulated liquid into a medium-size saucepan. Cover the grouper with aluminum foil and set aside.

To the liquid in the saucepan, add the remaining stick of butter, the mirin, brown sugar, asparagus, and mushrooms. Bring to a boil. Reduce the heat to low and cook for about 10 minutes, or until the vegetables begin to soften.

To serve, arrange the grouper on top of the sauce in a shallow serving bowl. Sprinkle with the Marley Coffee Spice Blend.

NOTE: Mirin, often used in Japanese cooking, is a low-alcohol sweet wine made from glutinous rice. It's widely available in supermarkets.

COFFEE-GRILLED LOIN LAMB CHOPS

YIELD: 4 SERVINGS

The marinade for this special dish contains the perfect ratio of garlic to sesame oil to hoisin to dark, rich brewed coffee. Grilled lamb chops are a real treat and the flavors in this recipe make them extra special.

INGREDIENTS

½ CUP (125 G) HOISIN SAUCE

¼ CUP (60 ML) BREWED BUFFALO SOLDIER COFFEE

3 CLOVES GARLIC, DICED

2 TABLESPOONS (30 ML) SESAME OIL, PLUS MORE FOR THE GRILL

JUICE OF 1 LIME

2 POUNDS (908 G) LOIN LAMB CHOPS

½ BUNCH FRESH CILANTRO, STEMMED AND CHOPPED, DIVIDED

1 TABLESPOON SESAME SEEDS, FOR GARNISH

DIRECTIONS

In a large, shallow bowl, whisk the hoisin, coffee, garlic, sesame oil, and lime juice. Add the lamb chops and half of the cilantro. Toss to coat both sides of the lamb. Set aside.

Preheat a well-cleaned grill to medium or place a grill pan over medium heat. Oil the grill with a little sesame oil. Arrange the lamb chops in a single layer on the grill and grill them for about 3 minutes. With a long-handled spatula, rotate the chops slightly so they develop attractive grill marks. Grill for 3 minutes more, flip the chops, and brush with any remaining hoisin mixture. Cook for 6 minutes more, rotating once more so grill marks develop. The chops should still be pink inside when done, with an internal temperature of 135°F (57°C). Transfer the chops to a serving platter. Sprinkle with the remaining cilantro and sesame seeds.

TIP: BE SURE YOUR GRILL IS SCRUPULOUSLY CLEAN BEFORE GRILLING THE CHOPS SO THEY LOOK GREAT, WITH PERFECT GRILL MARKS, WHEN FINISHED COOKING. NICE ACCOMPANIMENTS INCLUDE JASMINE RICE AND STIR-FRIED VEGETABLES.

CHAPTER

9

SALADS FROM AROUND THE WORLD

(Get Up, Stand Up coffee)

Coffee, when it is full-bodied and rich, like our Get Up, Stand Up coffee, contributes a lively flavor to a variety of crisp, colorful salads. In traditional vinaigrettes, coffee enhances the olive oil, the vinegar, and the fresh herbs in a very refreshing way. Tossing a green salad with a coffee-flavored vinaigrette lends an extra-special flavor to even the most ordinary of lettuces.

Grain salads, too, benefit from the hearty flavor of coffee. From an unusual Radish and Strawberry Salad with Coffee Vinaigrette (page 168) to a colorful Mango, Black Bean, and Avocado Salad (page 169) that will make you think you're in tropical paradise, these salads rely on fresh, colorful ingredients and are easy to pull off without a lot of effort.

Salad making is generally a low-stress cooking activity. Dressings can be made ahead of time, and greens can be washed, dried, and crisped well in advance. If you are making a salad that relies on pasta or whole grains, the main ingredient often can be prepped ahead and chilled until serving time. So get ready to reimagine your usual salads—and try some of these delicious options.

RADISH AND STRAWBERRY SALAD WITH COFFEE VINAIGRETTE

YIELD: 4 SERVINGS

Fresh ginger, coconut vinegar, a splash of coffee, and Dijon mustard make for a piquant dressing that is perfect tossed with fresh vegetables. Thanks to the red radishes, strawberries, and red onion, this salad is extra colorful and a feast for the eyes as well.

INGREDIENTS

FOR VINAIGRETTE:

1 TEASPOON DIJON MUSTARD

1 TABLESPOON (15 ML) AGAVE NECTAR

JUICE OF 1 LIME

¼ CUP (60 ML) COCONUT VINEGAR

¼ CUP (55 G) COCONUT OIL

¼ CUP (60 ML) BREWED, COOLED GET UP, STAND UP COFFEE

1 TEASPOON MINCED FRESH GINGER

FOR SALAD:

2 LARGE RADISHES, TRIMMED AND SLICED THIN

½ PINT (138 G) RED AND YELLOW CHERRY TOMATOES

1 PINT (290 G) STRAWBERRIES, WASHED, DRIED, HULLED, AND QUARTERED

¼ RED ONION, SLICED THIN

KOSHER SALT AND FRESHLY GROUND BLACK PEPPER TO TASTE

1 POUND (454 G) FRESH BABY SPINACH LEAVES OR OTHER FRESH GREENS, WASHED AND DRIED

FRESH HERBS, CHOPPED, FOR GARNISH (OPTIONAL)

DIRECTIONS

TO MAKE THE VINAIGRETTE:

In a medium-size bowl, whisk the mustard, agave nectar, lime juice, coconut vinegar, coconut oil, coffee, and ginger.

TO MAKE THE SALAD:

To the vinaigrette, add the radishes, cherry tomatoes, strawberries, and red onion. Toss until everything is well coated with dressing. Season with salt and pepper.

In a large serving bowl or decorative platter, arrange the spinach. Mound the dressed vegetables in the center. Garnish with chopped herbs, if desired. Serve immediately.

TIP: MAKE THE DRESSING UP TO 1 DAY IN ADVANCE AND REFRIGERATE IT, COVERED. TOSS WITH THE VEGETABLES JUST BEFORE SERVING.

MANGO, BLACK BEAN, AND AVOCADO SALAD

YIELD: 4 SERVINGS

The south-of-the-border flavor of this salad is enhanced by coffee—just enough to mellow and enrich the lively dressing.

INGREDIENTS

2 LARGE FRESH MANGOS, PEELED, PITTED, AND DICED

2 (14-OUNCE, OR 396 G) CANS BLACK BEANS, RINSED AND DRAINED

2 HASS AVOCADOS, PEELED, PITTED, AND DICED

½ PINT (138 G) RED AND/OR YELLOW CHERRY TOMATOES

2 CLOVES GARLIC, MINCED

1 BUNCH FRESH CILANTRO, STEMMED AND CHOPPED, DIVIDED

¼ CUP (60 ML) EXTRA-VIRGIN OLIVE OIL

¼ CUP (60 ML) COCONUT VINEGAR

1 TABLESPOON MARLEY COFFEE SPICE BLEND (PAGE 14)

1 MEDIUM-SIZE RED ONION, JULIENNED

KOSHER SALT AND FRESHLY GROUND BLACK PEPPER TO TASTE

½ POUND (225 G) FRISÉE, WASHED AND DRIED, OPTIONAL

LIME WEDGES, FOR GARNISH, OPTIONAL

DIRECTIONS

In a large bowl, combine the mangos, black beans, avocados, cherry tomatoes, garlic, half of the cilantro, olive oil, coconut vinegar, Marley Coffee Spice Blend, and red onion. Toss very well. Season with salt and pepper.

Arrange the frisée on a large platter or in a large serving bowl. Arrange the salad on top of the frisée. Garnish with the remaining cilantro and lime wedges.

TIP: DICE THE MANGOS AHEAD OF TIME IF YOU LIKE, BUT WAIT UNTIL THE LAST MINUTE TO PREP THE AVOCADOS SO THEY RETAIN THEIR COLOR AND FLAVOR.

COFFEE-INFUSED CHINESE CHICKEN SALAD WITH MANDARIN ❧ ORANGE-CASHEW DRESSING ❧

YIELD: 4 SERVINGS

When paired with other assertive ingredients, such as fresh ginger and rice wine vinegar, the coffee in this dressing delivers a punch of lively flavor. Crunchy, colorful, and satisfying, this festive main course is loaded with vegetables.

INGREDIENTS

FOR DRESSING:

½ CUP (120 ML) EXTRA-VIRGIN OLIVE OIL

½ CUP (57 G) CANNED MANDARIN ORANGE SEGMENTS, DRAINED

½ CUP (69 G) CASHEWS

¼ CUP (60 ML) AGAVE NECTAR

¼ CUP (60 ML) BREWED, COOLED GET UP, STAND UP COFFEE

2 TABLESPOONS (30 ML) SESAME OIL

2 TABLESPOONS (30 ML) RICE WINE VINEGAR

1 SHALLOT, DICED

1 CLOVE GARLIC, MINCED

1 TEASPOON CHOPPED FRESH GINGER

KOSHER SALT AND FRESHLY GROUND BLACK PEPPER TO TASTE

FOR SALAD:

1 TABLESPOON (15 ML) LOW-SODIUM SOY SAUCE

½ TEASPOON SESAME OIL

4 (4-OUNCE, OR 115 G) PORTIONS OF BONELESS, SKINLESS CHICKEN BREASTS

2 HEADS ROMAINE LETTUCE, WASHED AND PATTED DRY

1 CUP (70 G) JULIENNED NAPA CABBAGE

1 SCALLION (WHITE AND LIGHT GREEN PARTS), CHOPPED

¼ CUP (40 G) JULIENNED RED ONION

¼ CUP (18 G) JULIENNED RED CABBAGE

¼ CUP (28 G) SHREDDED CARROT

¼ CUP (16 G) HALVED SNOW PEAS

¼ CUP (37 G) EDAMAME, THAWED IF FROZEN

1 TEASPOON BLACK SESAME SEEDS

DIRECTIONS

TO MAKE THE DRESSING:

In a blender, combine the olive oil, mandarin oranges, cashews, agave nectar, coffee, sesame oil, rice wine vinegar, shallot, garlic, and ginger. Blend at medium speed for about 2 minutes, or until all ingredients are well incorporated. Season with salt and pepper. Cover and set aside.

TO MAKE THE SALAD:

In a medium-size bowl, combine the soy sauce and sesame oil. Add the chicken and turn to coat.

Preheat a grill pan over medium heat. Grill the chicken for about 3 minutes per side, or until cooked through with no pink remaining. Set aside.

In a large bowl, combine the romaine lettuce, napa cabbage, scallion, red onion, red cabbage, carrot, snow peas, edamame, and sesame seeds. Slice the chicken and add it to the bowl. Toss the salad with the dressing. Divide the salad among 4 large bowls.

TIP: IF YOU PREFER, SERVE THE DRESSING ON THE SIDE AND LET EVERYONE ADD AS MUCH AS THEY LIKE.

WATERMELON, FETA,
❧ AND CUCUMBER SALAD ❧

YIELD: 6 SERVINGS

A colorful and zesty salad that begs to be made in summer, when tomatoes and watermelons are at their peak. This has a lovely champagne vinaigrette subtly enhanced with a hit of richly flavored coffee.

INGREDIENTS

3 TABLESPOONS (45 ML) EXTRA-VIRGIN OLIVE OIL

2 TABLESPOONS (30 ML) CHAMPAGNE VINEGAR

2 CLOVES GARLIC, MINCED

½ TEASPOON KOSHER SALT

FRESHLY GROUND BLACK PEPPER TO TASTE

JUICE OF ½ LEMON

GRATED ZEST OF 1 LEMON

2 TABLESPOONS (26 G) SUGAR

¼ CUP (60 ML) BREWED, CHILLED GET UP, STAND UP COFFEE

4 FRESH MINT LEAVES, CHOPPED

3 FRESH BASIL LEAVES, CHOPPED

2 CUPS (300 G) CHERRY TOMATOES

½ MEDIUM-SIZE SEEDLESS WATERMELON, SEEDED AND DICED

½ POUND (225 G) ARUGULA, TRIMMED AND TORN INTO BITE-SIZE LEAVES

1 EUROPEAN CUCUMBER, SLICED THIN

¼ SMALL RED ONION, SLICED

¼ CUP (38 G) FETA CHEESE, CRUMBLED

DIRECTIONS

In a large serving bowl, whisk the olive oil, vinegar, garlic, salt, pepper, lemon juice, lemon zest, sugar, coffee, mint, and basil until thick and creamy.

Add the tomatoes, watermelon, arugula, cucumber, and red onion. Toss gently so the dressing coats all the ingredients. Top with the feta cheese.

TIP: THIS DELICIOUS SALAD IS BEST SERVED SOON AFTER BEING MADE, BUT THE DRESSING CAN BE PREPARED AHEAD OF TIME.

INDIAN COUSCOUS SALAD WITH
❧ COFFEE VINAIGRETTE ❧

YIELD: 4 TO 6 SERVINGS

Coffee brings out the best in this exotic and colorful salad, which is delicious served with your favorite chicken or seafood dish.

INGREDIENTS

3 CUPS (705 ML) VEGETABLE STOCK OR BROTH

1 HEAPING TEASPOON (1 G) SAFFRON THREADS

PINCH SALT

6 TABLESPOONS (90 ML) EXTRA-VIRGIN OLIVE OIL, DIVIDED

1 POUND (454 G) ISRAELI COUSCOUS

2 TABLESPOONS CURRY POWDER

8 YELLOW CHERRY TOMATOES, HALVED

8 RED CHERRY TOMATOES, HALVED

¼ RED ONION, DICED

¼ BUNCH FRESH CILANTRO, STEMMED AND CHOPPED

1 TABLESPOON MARLEY COFFEE SPICE BLEND (PAGE 14)

⅓ CUP MICROGREENS

KOSHER SALT AND FRESHLY GROUND BLACK PEPPER TO TASTE

RAINBOW MICROGREENS, FOR GARNISH (OPTIONAL)

DIRECTIONS

In a large saucepan over high heat, bring the vegetable stock to a boil. Stir in the saffron, salt, and 3 tablespoons (45 ml) olive oil. Add the couscous, stir, reduce the heat to low, and cook for 5 minutes. Drain the couscous through a fine chinois. Transfer it to a large serving bowl.

Add the curry powder, yellow and red tomatoes, red onion, cilantro, Marley Coffee Spice Blend, and microgreens. Toss with the remaining 3 tablespoons (45 ml) olive oil. Season with salt and pepper. Refrigerate for at least 30 minutes before serving. Garnish with rainbow microgreens, if desired.

NOTE: Israeli couscous consists of granules, made from semolina and wheat flour, about the size of small pearls. It's chewier and nuttier than regular couscous and makes an ideal salad ingredient.

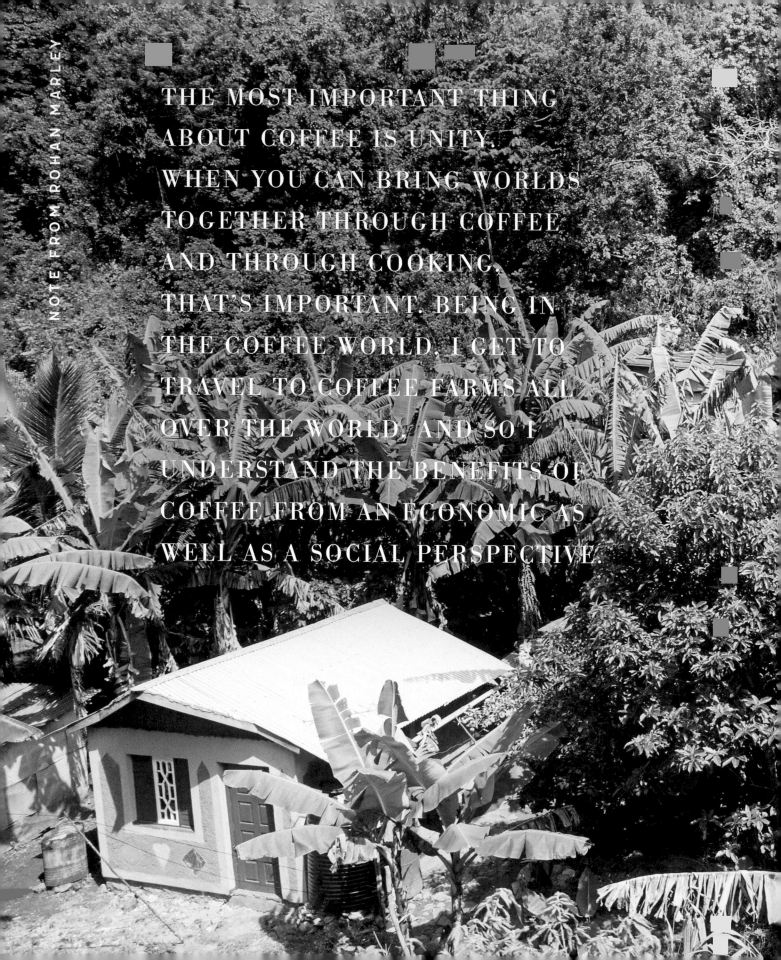

THE MOST IMPORTANT THING
ABOUT COFFEE IS UNITY.
WHEN YOU CAN BRING WORLDS
TOGETHER THROUGH COFFEE
AND THROUGH COOKING,
THAT'S IMPORTANT. BEING IN
THE COFFEE WORLD, I GET TO
TRAVEL TO COFFEE FARMS ALL
OVER THE WORLD, AND SO I
UNDERSTAND THE BENEFITS OF
COFFEE FROM AN ECONOMIC AS
WELL AS A SOCIAL PERSPECTIVE.

❧

FRIED PLANTAINS

YIELD: 4 TO 6 SERVINGS

This is a delicious, hearty addition to a variety of meat and poultry-based meals, and it's incredibly easy to make.

INGREDIENTS

½ CUP (109 G) COCONUT OIL

2 LARGE, RIPE PLANTAINS, PEELED AND SLICED

KOSHER SALT TO TASTE

2 TABLESPOONS (ABOUT 24 G) MARLEY COFFEE SPICE BLEND
    (PAGE 14)

DIRECTIONS

In a large, heavy skillet or sauté pan over medium-high heat, heat the coconut oil until very hot. Carefully place the plantain slices in the oil, and sear them for about 2 minutes per side, or until they start to color. Transfer to a serving platter, sprinkle with salt and Marley Coffee Spice Blend, and serve hot.

NOTE: Plantains can range in color from brownish-black to green to yellow. Larger and firmer than regular bananas, plantains have a mild flavor not dissimilar to squash.

LO MEIN SALAD WITH
❖ COFFEE-PEANUT DRESSING ❖

YIELD: 4 SERVINGS

Dress this crunchy, colorful Asian noodle salad with coffee-infused dressing and serve as a light lunch or dinner side. This make-ahead dish is ideal for picnics, too.

INGREDIENTS

FOR DRESSING:

4 TABLESPOONS (65 G) PEANUT BUTTER

¼ CUP (60 ML) SESAME OIL

¼ CUP (60 ML) LOW-SODIUM SOY SAUCE

¼ CUP (60 ML) BREWED, COOLED GET UP, STAND UP COFFEE

2 TABLESPOONS (40 G) HONEY

JUICE OF 1 LIME

1 TEASPOON MINCED FRESH GINGER

FOR SALAD:

1 TABLESPOON (15 ML) SESAME OIL

1 POUND (454 G) LO MEIN NOODLES

1 CUP (70 G) SHREDDED RED CABBAGE

¼ CUP (25 G) SLICED SCALLIONS

¼ CUP (37 G) EDAMAME, THAWED IF FROZEN

½ CUP (55 G) SHREDDED CARROT (ABOUT 1 LARGE CARROT)

2 TABLESPOONS (16 G) SESAME SEEDS

FRIED WONTON CRISPS

DIRECTIONS

TO MAKE THE DRESSING:

In a small bowl, whisk the peanut butter, sesame oil, soy sauce, coffee, honey, lime juice, and ginger for 1 minute, or until the dressing is emulsified.

TO MAKE THE SALAD:

Bring a large saucepan of water to a boil over high heat. Add the sesame oil and lo mein noodles. Cook the noodles according to the package directions—typically for about 5 minutes. Drain the noodles and run them under cold water. Drain again. Transfer to a large serving bowl.

Add the red cabbage, scallions, edamame, carrot, and sesame seeds. Pour on the dressing and toss gently until the noodles are completely coated. Top with fried wonton crisps.

CHAPTER

10

SWEETS AND TREATS

(Simmer Down coffee)

Dessert and coffee are a natural pairing. The best meals end with a sweet treat and a mug of coffee, a tiny demitasse of espresso, or perhaps a cinnamon-dusted latte. And many people finish a meal with a coffee-based drink that actually *is* dessert. (Yes, a coffee milkshake definitely counts here!) Now consider the delicious idea of stirring coffee *into* desserts—cakes, ice cream, pies, cookies—and prepare for some sweet surprises. Simmer Down, the rich-tasting decaffeinated Marley coffee, is ideal to use in desserts for those trying to avoid caffeine. But the coffee you choose for any dessert in this collection is really a matter of personal preference.

These desserts range from elegant—Espresso–Grand Marnier Balls with Vanilla Ice Cream (page 189)—to homey—Apple Bread Pudding with a Coffee-Rum Sauce (page 186). Classics such as pecan pie and Key lime pie feel more contemporary when featuring a coffee-infused crust. Of course, there's plenty here for chocolate lovers, too, like Salted Caramel Coffee Brownies (page 192) and a rich Chocolate Lava Cake (page 196).

In these and other desserts, the coffee flavor is subtle, contributing just a bit of richness and enhancing the rum, caramel, or chocolate that goes into the dessert.

COFFEE OIL–INFUSED BUTTER CAKE
❧ WITH BLACKBERRY COMPOTE ❧

YIELD: 12 SERVINGS

A classic cake with a tender crumb and lovely flavor from coffee-infused oil, this is especially good when served with the fresh blackberry compote. Not overly sweet, this cake also would be good on its own—with a cup of coffee, of course! Dessert is served.

INGREDIENTS

FOR BLACKBERRY COMPOTE:

2 CUPS (290 G) FRESH BLACKBERRIES

¼ CUP (50 G) SUGAR

2 TABLESPOONS (30 ML) FRESHLY SQUEEZED LEMON JUICE

½ TEASPOON FRESHLY GRATED LEMON ZEST

FOR CAKE:

½ POUND (2 STICKS, OR 225 G) UNSALTED BUTTER, AT ROOM TEMPERATURE, PLUS MORE FOR PREPARING THE CAKE PANS

3 CUPS (336 G) ALL-PURPOSE FLOUR, PLUS MORE FOR DUSTING THE CAKE PANS

1 TABLESPOON BAKING POWDER

½ TEASPOON SALT

1¼ CUPS (250 G) SUGAR

4 EGGS

1¼ CUPS (285 ML) WHOLE MILK

1 TABLESPOON (15 ML) VANILLA EXTRACT

2 TABLESPOONS (30 ML) COFFEE AND STAR ANISE-INFUSED OIL (PAGE 24)

TIP: YOU MAY PREPARE THE COMPOTE A DAY OR TWO IN ADVANCE. REFRIGERATE, TIGHTLY COVERED. ALSO, YOU MAY BAKE THIS CAKE IN A LARGE BUNDT PAN INSTEAD OF TWO ROUND LAYER PANS IF YOU LIKE.

DIRECTIONS

TO MAKE THE COMPOTE:

In a medium-size saucepan over medium heat, combine the blackberries, sugar, lemon juice, and lemon zest. Bring to a boil, stirring. Reduce the heat to low and simmer for 10 to 15 minutes, stirring occasionally, or until the compote starts to thicken. Remove from the heat, transfer to a small bowl, and cool. Cover with plastic wrap.

TO MAKE THE CAKE:

Preheat the oven to 350° F (180°C, or gas mark 4). Lightly butter two 9-inch (23 cm) round cake pans. Dust lightly with flour.

In a medium-size bowl, whisk the flour, baking powder, and salt.

In a large bowl, with an electric mixer set at medium speed, beat the butter with the sugar for 3 minutes, or until light and fluffy. Reduce the mixer speed to low and beat in the eggs, one at a time.

Alternating ingredients, add the flour and milk to the creamed mixture, about one-third of each at a time, and beat after each addition just until the batter is smooth. Beat in the vanilla and the infused oil. Evenly divide the batter between the 2 prepared pans, smoothing the tops.

Bake for about 30 minutes, or until the top of each cake springs back when pressed with your finger and a cake tester inserted into the center of the cake comes out clean. Remove the pans from the oven. Cool the cakes in the pan for 15 minutes. Run a knife around the edges of each pan to loosen the cake. Invert the cakes onto a platter and set aside to cool completely. Slice the cake into pieces and serve with the compote.

PECAN PIE
❧ WITH ALMOND-COFFEE CRUST ❧

YIELD: 6 TO 8 SERVINGS

Coffee in both the crust and filling of this traditional pie adds subtle flavor. Top with softly whipped cream if you like, and be prepared for recipe requests.

INGREDIENTS

FOR CRUST:

2 CUPS (224 G) ALL-PURPOSE FLOUR

1 CUP (96 G) ALMOND FLOUR

¼ CUP (50 G) SUGAR

1 TABLESPOON FINELY GROUND SIMMER DOWN COFFEE BEANS

PINCH SALT

⅓ CUP (75 G) CHILLED UNSALTED BUTTER

⅓ CUP (67 G) CHILLED SHORTENING

1 CUP (235 ML) COLD WATER

FOR FILLING:

1 CUP (235 ML) DARK CORN SYRUP

1 CUP (200 G) SUGAR

3 EGGS, LIGHTLY BEATEN

2 TABLESPOONS (30 ML) MELTED UNSALTED BUTTER

1 TEASPOON (5 ML) VANILLA EXTRACT

PINCH SALT

1½ CUPS (150 G) PECANS

DIRECTIONS

TO MAKE THE CRUST:

In a large bowl, mix the all-purpose flour, almond flour, sugar, ground coffee beans, and salt. Add the butter and shortening. Using a pastry cutter or fork, cut the butter and shortening into the flour mixture until it resembles coarse crumbs.

Add the water a little at a time, stirring the dough with your fingertips as you pour. (Don't use your palms. They tend to warm the dough too much.) Add a bit more water if the dough seems too dry. When the dough comes together nicely, form it into 2 balls, wrap each in plastic wrap, and chill them for at least 1 hour.

Preheat the oven to 350°F (180°C, or gas mark 4). On a lightly floured surface, roll out one dough ball to a 9-inch (23 cm) circle. Transfer to a 9-inch (23 cm) pie plate. Press the dough into the pie plate and crimp the edges.

TO MAKE THE FILLING:

In a large bowl, whisk the corn syrup, sugar, eggs, butter, vanilla, and salt. When well mixed, stir in the pecans. Pour the filling into the prepared pie shell. Bake for 45 minutes, or until the crust is nicely brown and the filling is set. Serve warm or chilled.

TIP: THIS RECIPE MAKES ENOUGH DOUGH FOR TWO CRUSTS. KEEP THE EXTRA DOUGH REFRIGERATED FOR 1 WEEK OR FREEZE FOR UP TO 2 MONTHS.

APPLE BREAD PUDDING WITH A COFFEE-RUM SAUCE

YIELD: 8 SERVINGS

A delicious, caramel-like sauce tempered with rum and coffee takes this traditional apple bread pudding to a sumptuous level. The pudding, not too sweet, is loaded with spices and diced apple. If you have leftovers, seriously consider eating them for breakfast.

INGREDIENTS

UNSALTED BUTTER, FOR PREPARING THE BAKING PAN

FOR APPLE MIXTURE:

3 GRANNY SMITH APPLES, PEELED, CORED, AND DICED

JUICE OF 1/2 LEMON

2 TABLESPOONS (28 G) UNSALTED BUTTER

1/4 CUP (50 G) SUGAR

1 TEASPOON GROUND CINNAMON

1/2 TEASPOON GROUND NUTMEG

1/4 TEASPOON GROUND CLOVES

FOR BREAD MIXTURE:

1 LOAF DAY-OLD BREAD, TORN INTO BITE-SIZE PIECES

1 CUP (200 G) SUGAR

1 CUP (235 ML) WHOLE MILK, PLUS MORE AS NEEDED

1 1/2 TEASPOONS GROUND CINNAMON

1/2 TEASPOON GROUND NUTMEG

1/4 TEASPOON GROUND CLOVES

1 TEASPOON (5 ML) VANILLA EXTRACT

1 CUP (145 G) RAISINS

FOR COFFEE-RUM SAUCE:

1/2 CUP (1 STICK, OR 113 G) UNSALTED BUTTER

1 CUP (225 G) PACKED LIGHT BROWN SUGAR

1/2 CUP (120 ML) HEAVY CREAM

1 TABLESPOON (15 ML) LIGHT OR DARK RUM, PREFERABLY MARLEY BRAND

1 TABLESPOON (15 ML) STRONG BREWED SIMMER DOWN COFFEE

DIRECTIONS

Preheat the oven to 350°F (180°C, or gas mark 4). Butter a 9 x 13-inch (23 x 33 cm) baking pan.

TO MAKE THE APPLE MIXTURE:

Place the diced apples in a medium-size bowl and squeeze the lemon juice over. (This keeps them from turning brown.) In a medium-size saucepan over medium heat, melt the butter. Add the apples, sugar, cinnamon, nutmeg, and cloves. Reduce the heat to low and cook for 5 to 8 minutes, or until thick and the apples begin to soften. Remove from the heat and set aside.

TO MAKE THE BREAD MIXTURE:

In a large bowl, stir together the bread, sugar, milk, cinnamon, nutmeg, cloves, vanilla, and raisins. Stir in the apple mixture and mix well. If the mixture seems dry, add milk, 1 tablespoon (15 ml) at a time, until all the bread is moist. Transfer to the prepared pan and bake for 20 to 30 minutes, or until very hot and the top is golden brown.

MEANWHILE, MAKE THE COFFEE-RUM SAUCE:

In a medium-size saucepan over medium heat, cook the butter and brown sugar until the butter melts and the mixture is smooth.

Reduce the heat to low and cook for about 2 minutes, stirring. Stir in the heavy cream, rum, and coffee. Bring to a simmer. Cook for 5 minutes, stirring often, or until thick. Remove from the heat and let cool for 10 minutes.

Cut the bread pudding into 8 portions and drizzle with sauce.

TIP: MAKE THE SAUCE A DAY AHEAD AND KEEP REFRIGERATED, COVERED. LEFTOVER SAUCE IS DELICIOUS ON YOUR FAVORITE ICE CREAM.

COFFEE-SPICED BANANA BREAD PUDDING
❧ WITH CARAMEL-RUM SAUCE ❧

YIELD: 8 TO 10 SERVINGS

Overtones of sweet spices and a rich, full-bodied coffee flavor enliven this extraordinarily good and easy-to-make bread pudding. The vanilla pairs perfectly with mellow Simmer Down coffee in this delicious spin on a classic dessert.

INGREDIENTS

UNSALTED BUTTER, FOR COATING THE BAKING DISH

FOR PUDDING:

6 EGGS

1 CUP (235 ML) BREWED, COOLED SIMMER DOWN COFFEE

¼ CUP (60 ML) AGAVE NECTAR

3 TABLESPOONS (45 ML) VANILLA EXTRACT

2 LOAVES CHALLAH BREAD, CUBED

3 TABLESPOONS (17 G) PUMPKIN PIE SPICE

¼ POUND (1 STICK, OR 113 G) UNSALTED BUTTER, SOFTENED AND CUBED

2 LARGE RIPE BANANAS, ROUGHLY CHOPPED

FOR CARAMEL-RUM SAUCE:

½ CUP (120 ML) CARAMEL SAUCE

3 TABLESPOONS (45 ML) BREWED, COOLED SIMMER DOWN COFFEE

2 TABLESPOONS (30 ML) DARK RUM, PREFERABLY MARLEY BRAND

DIRECTIONS

Preheat the oven to 375°F (190°C, or gas mark 5) and lightly butter a square or rectangular 2-quart baking dish.

TO MAKE THE PUDDING:

In a large bowl, whisk the eggs until foamy. Add the coffee, agave nectar, and vanilla. Whisk well. Fold in the challah. Add the pumpkin pie spice, butter, and bananas. Toss well. Transfer to the prepared dish and bake for 45 minutes, uncovered, until firm to the touch and a toothpick inserted into the center comes out clean.

TO MAKE THE CARAMEL-RUM SAUCE:

In a small bowl, stir together the caramel sauce, coffee, and rum. Serve the pudding warm, topped with the sauce.

TIP: USE YOUR FAVORITE CARAMEL SAUCE FOR THIS RECIPE. LEFTOVER CARAMEL-RUM SAUCE WILL KEEP, REFRIGERATED AND TIGHTLY COVERED, FOR AT LEAST 1 WEEK.

ESPRESSO-GRAND MARNIER BALLS ❧ WITH VANILLA ICE CREAM ❧

YIELD: 4 TO 6 SERVINGS

This rich dessert will satisfy the most diehard chocoholics, who may opt for chocolate ice cream on top.

INGREDIENTS

FOR BALLS:

2/3 CUP (156.5 ML) HEAVY CREAM

5 TABLESPOONS (70 G) UNSALTED BUTTER

10 OUNCES (280 G) BITTERSWEET CHOCOLATE, FINELY CHOPPED

2 TABLESPOONS (30 ML) ORANGE-FLAVORED LIQUEUR, SUCH AS GRAND MARNIER

2 TABLESPOONS (30 ML) BREWED SIMMER DOWN COFFEE

FOR COATING:

5 OUNCES (140 G) SEMI-SWEET CHOCOLATE

1 TEASPOON COCONUT OIL

4 TABLESPOONS (20 G) FINELY GROUND SIMMER DOWN COFFEE

FOR ICE CREAM:

2 CUPS (475 ML) WHOLE MILK

1 VANILLA BEAN, HALVED, SEEDS SCRAPED OUT AND RESERVED

1/4 CUP (50 G) SUGAR

5 EGG YOLKS

DIRECTIONS

TO MAKE THE BALLS:

In a medium-size heavy saucepan over medium heat, combine the heavy cream and butter. Cook until scalding (just below a boil), stirring. Reduce heat to low and add the bittersweet chocolate. Whisk until very thick. Stir in the liqueur and coffee and pour the mixture into a heatproof bowl. Cover and refrigerate for 2 hours, or until firm.

With a small scoop or melon baller, scoop out 12 to 15 balls of the mixture. Arrange them on a parchment paper–lined tray and refrigerate for another hour, or until firm.

MEANWHILE, MAKE THE COATING:

In a small heatproof bowl or saucepan, melt the semi-sweet chocolate and coconut oil over low heat. Whisk until smooth. Remove from the heat. Using 2 forks to hold each chilled ball, dip them into the melted chocolate. Place them on the parchment paper and sprinkle with the coffee. Refrigerate to harden for at least 30 minutes. Remove them from the refrigerator about 20 minutes before serving.

TO MAKE THE ICE CREAM:

In a medium-size saucepan over medium heat, bring the milk, vanilla bean halves, and vanilla seeds to a simmer. Remove from the heat and set aside for 10 minutes so the milk absorbs the vanilla flavor.

Meanwhile, in a medium-size bowl, whisk the sugar and egg yolks until frothy. Whisking constantly to avoid scrambling the eggs, slowly drizzle half of the hot milk mixture into the egg mixture. Return the mixture to the saucepan over very low heat and cook for 10 to 15 minutes, whisking, until the mixture coats the back of a spoon. Pour the mixture into a heatproof bowl, place plastic wrap on top, and press down so condensation cannot form. Refrigerate for 4 hours. Transfer the cooled mixture to an ice cream maker and follow the manufacturer's instructions. Serve the balls with the vanilla ice cream.

TIP: NOT SURE THE BALL MIXTURE IS COOKED? WHILE IT'S STILL IN THE PAN, DIP A SPOON INTO THE CUSTARD. IF THE BACK OF THE SPOON IS COATED, RUN YOUR FINGER THROUGH THE MIXTURE. IF YOU MAKE A CLEAN LINE, THE MIXTURE IS READY FOR THE HEATPROOF BOWL.

WHEN CHEF MAX TOLD ME ALL THE FOODS YOU COULD MAKE TASTE BETTER WITH COFFEE, I THOUGHT HOW WONDERFUL IT IS TO BE ABLE TO USE COFFEE IN THIS WAY. BUT FOR ME, COFFEE IN DESSERT IS ALWAYS NICE. I LIKE TO HAVE A CARAMEL-FLAVORED COFFEE ALONG WITH DESSERT. IT'S JUST A WONDERFUL WAY TO END THE MEAL. AND A DESSERT WITH COFFEE IN IT IS REALLY SPECIAL.

❖ SALTED CARAMEL–COFFEE BROWNIES ❖

YIELD: 12 BROWNIES

Rich and chocolaty, this is an unusually good brownie thanks to the finely ground coffee beans in the batter and the homemade caramel on top. It's finished off with a sprinkling of flaky sea salt—truly indulgent!

INGREDIENTS

FOR BROWNIES:

½ CUP (1 STICK, OR 113 G) UNSALTED BUTTER, PLUS MORE FOR PREPARING THE BAKING PAN

¾ CUP (84 G) ALL-PURPOSE FLOUR, PLUS MORE FOR DUSTING THE BAKING PAN

1 CUP (225 G) PACKED DARK BROWN SUGAR

4 OUNCES (115 G) BITTERSWEET CHOCOLATE, CHOPPED

1 TABLESPOON FINELY GROUND SIMMER DOWN COFFEE BEANS

1 EGG

1 TABLESPOON (15 ML) VANILLA EXTRACT

¼ TEASPOON BAKING POWDER

PINCH KOSHER SALT

FOR CARAMEL:

1 CUP (225 G) PACKED LIGHT BROWN SUGAR

7 TABLESPOONS (98 G) UNSALTED BUTTER

½ CUP (120 ML) HEAVY CREAM

FOR TOPPING:

1 TABLESPOON (18 G) FLAKY SEA SALT

DIRECTIONS

TO MAKE THE BROWNIES:

Preheat the oven to 350°F (180°C, or gas mark 4). Butter and flour an 8 x 8-inch (20 x 20 cm) baking pan. In a microwave-safe bowl, combine the brown sugar, butter, bittersweet chocolate, and coffee. Microwave at medium temperature for 1 or 2 minutes. Stir and microwave again for another minute. Repeat until the chocolate and butter are melted and the mixture is well combined. Let cool for 10 minutes.

Whisk in the egg and vanilla. Add the flour, baking powder, and salt and mix very well. Spoon and scrape the mixture into the prepared pan. Bake for 25 to 30 minutes, or until a toothpick inserted into the center comes out with a little fudgy dough on the end. The dough should not look wet. Let cool in the pan for 15 minutes.

TO MAKE THE CARAMEL:

In a medium-size saucepan over low heat, combine the brown sugar, butter, and heavy cream. Cook, stirring, until thick and smooth.

Drizzle the caramel over the brownies and sprinkle the top with sea salt. Cool and cut into 12 squares.

TIP: THESE BROWNIES MAY BE FROZEN, WELL WRAPPED, FOR UP TO 3 MONTHS.

❧ HAZELNUT-ESPRESSO ICE CREAM ❧

YIELD: 6 TO 8 SERVINGS

Coffee and hazelnuts make for a winning flavor duo in ice cream, and this homemade version is richly satisfying without being cloyingly sweet.

INGREDIENTS

2 CUPS (475 ML) WHOLE MILK

1 VANILLA BEAN, HALVED, SEEDS SCRAPED OUT AND RESERVED

2 TABLESPOONS VERY FINELY GROUND SIMMER DOWN COFFEE BEANS

¼ CUP (50 G) SUGAR

5 EGG YOLKS

1 CUP (115 G) CHOPPED HAZELNUTS

DIRECTIONS

In a medium-size, heavy saucepan bring the milk, vanilla bean halves, and vanilla seeds to a simmer. Remove from the heat and set aside for 10 minutes to steep. Let cool slightly.

In a medium-size bowl, whisk the sugar and egg yolks until frothy. While whisking, slowly drizzle in half of the hot milk to temper the eggs, but not scramble them. Pour in the remaining hot milk. Return the mixture to the pan and place it over medium-low heat. Cook for 10 to 15 minutes, whisking, until the mixture thickens and coats the back of a spoon. To test for readiness, dip a spoon into the mixture and run your finger over the back of the spoon. If you can make a clean line, it's ready. Pour it into a heatproof bowl and cover with plastic wrap, pressing down on the wrap so there is no space for condensation to form. Refrigerate for 4 hours.

Pour the chilled mixture into an ice cream maker and follow the manufacturer's instructions for freezing. During the last 5 or 10 minutes of churning, add the hazelnuts. Continue to churn until ready. Transfer to a freezer-safe bowl and freeze for at least 2 hours, or until firm.

NOTE: If you buy hazelnuts in the shell, be aware that you'll get about 1½ cups (203 g) of hazelnuts for every pound (454 g) of hazelnuts in the shell.

KEY LIME PIE WITH COFFEE-GRAHAM CRACKER CRUST

YIELD: 1 PIE OR 6 INDIVIDUAL SERVINGS

Undertones of coffee cut the crust's sweetness just enough so it complements the filling's tanginess. This is the perfect dessert to make ahead, chill, and pull out to impress your dinner guests.

INGREDIENTS

FOR CRUST:

1½ CUPS (90 G) GRAHAM CRACKER CRUMBS

½ CUP (1 STICK, OR 113 G) MELTED UNSALTED BUTTER

2 TABLESPOONS VERY FINELY GROUND SIMMER DOWN COFFEE BEANS

FOR FILLING:

3 EGG YOLKS

1 (14-OUNCE OR 396 G) CAN SWEETENED CONDENSED MILK

4 TEASPOONS FINELY GRATED KEY LIME ZEST, PLUS MORE FOR GARNISH

½ CUP (120 ML) KEY LIME JUICE

KEY LIME SLICES FOR GARNISH (OPTIONAL)

DIRECTIONS

Preheat the oven to 350°F (180°C, or gas mark 4).

TO MAKE THE CRUST:

In a medium-size bowl, mix the graham cracker crumbs, butter, and coffee. Transfer to a 9-inch (23 cm) pie dish or divide between six 3-inch (8 cm) tart pans, pressing firmly onto the bottom and up the sides. Bake for 10 minutes.

TO MAKE THE FILLING:

In the work bowl of an electric mixer, using the wire whisk attachment, whisk the egg yolks for about 2 minutes. Add the condensed milk and beat for 1 minute more, scraping down the sides of the bowl with a spatula a couple of times. Add the lime zest and beat briefly. With the mixer set at low speed, drizzle in the lime juice and whisk for 1 minute. Pour the filling into the crust(s) and bake for 15 minutes, or until set. Cool completely on a wire rack. Refrigerate for at least 2 hours before serving. Garnish with lime zest and slices, if desired.

TIP: DON'T OVERBAKE THIS PIE OR THE CRUST WILL BECOME TOO HARD. WHIPPED CREAM, WHILE OPTIONAL, DRESSES UP THIS DESSERT BEAUTIFULLY.

CHOCOLATE LAVA CAKES WITH ESPRESSO CRÈME ANGLAISE

YIELD: 12 CAKES

This classic, rich French custard sauce that gilds so many cakes and fruits is deliciously infused with flavorful ground coffee beans and served with a hard to resist soft-centered chocolate cake. You can make the crème anglaise ahead of time and keep it, tightly covered, in the refrigerator until ready to use.

INGREDIENTS

FOR CRÈME ANGLAISE:

2 CUPS (475 ML) WHOLE MILK

1 VANILLA BEAN, HALVED, SEEDS SCRAPED OUT AND RESERVED

2 TABLESPOONS FINELY GROUND SIMMER DOWN COFFEE BEANS

¼ CUP (50 G) SUGAR

5 EGG YOLKS

FOR CAKES:

7 OUNCES (195 G) BITTERSWEET CHOCOLATE, FINELY CHOPPED

⅓ CUP (75 G) UNSALTED BUTTER

4 EGGS

⅓ CUP (67 G) SUGAR

⅓ CUP (37 G) ALL-PURPOSE FLOUR

DIRECTIONS

TO MAKE THE CRÈME ANGLAISE:

In a heavy saucepan over low heat, bring the milk, vanilla bean halves and seeds, and coffee to a simmer. Remove from the heat and set aside for 10 minutes to steep. Remove the vanilla bean halves.

Meanwhile, in a mixing bowl, whisk the sugar and egg yolks until frothy. While whisking, slowly drizzle half of the hot milk mixture into the yolk mixture to temper the eggs, not scramble them. Pour in the remaining hot milk and place the pan over low heat. Cook the mixture for 6 to 8 minutes, or until thickened and it coats the back of a spoon. To test if it's ready, dip the spoon into the mixture and run your finger over the back of the spoon. If you can make a clean line, it's ready. Remove the crème anglaise from the heat and set aside.

TO MAKE THE CAKES:

Preheat the oven to 400°F (200°C, or gas mark 6). In the top of a double boiler, melt the chocolate and butter. Set aside to cool slightly.

In a medium-size bowl, whisk the eggs and sugar until foamy and pale-colored. Slowly stir the egg mixture into the cooled chocolate mixture. Stir in the flour and mix well. If the batter is very runny, add another tablespoon of flour. Fill 12 2- or 3-ounce ramekins with the batter, filling each about three-fourths full. Place the ramekins on a baking sheet and bake for about 7 minutes, or until the tops spring back when touched with your finger. Remove the cakes from the ramekins, centering 1 on each serving plate, and drizzle with crème anglaise.

TIP: DON'T OVERBAKE THESE CAKES. THEY'RE SUPPOSED TO BE A LITTLE RUNNY ON THE INSIDE, BUT IF YOU PREFER A FIRMER CONSISTENCY, LEAVE THEM IN THE OVEN FOR A FEW EXTRA MINUTES.

SWEETS AND TREATS

COFFEE-INFUSED OATMEAL COOKIES
❖ WITH CANNOLI CREAM FILLING ❖

YIELD: 6 TO 8 SANDWICH COOKIES

If you love cannoli, you will fall for these amazing home-made oatmeal cookies, which are sandwiched together with cannoli cream filling. This filling has just a hint of finely ground espresso coffee beans that cuts the sweetness and enhances its creaminess. Adding chocolate chips is like gilding the lily.

INGREDIENTS

FOR COOKIES:

½ CUP (1 STICK, OR 113 G) SOFTENED UNSALTED BUTTER

½ CUP (100 G) GRANULATED SUGAR

½ CUP (120 G) PACKED LIGHT BROWN SUGAR

1 EGG

3 TABLESPOONS (45 ML) BREWED, COOLED SIMMER DOWN COFFEE

1 TEASPOON (5 ML) VANILLA EXTRACT

1 CUP (112 G) ALL-PURPOSE FLOUR

1½ CUPS (234 G) OLD-FASHIONED ROLLED OATS (NOT INSTANT)

1 TEASPOON BAKING SODA

1 TEASPOON GROUND CINNAMON

½ TEASPOON GROUND NUTMEG

½ TEASPOON GROUND CLOVES

PINCH SALT

FOR CANNOLI CREAM FILLING:

1 CUP (25 G) RICOTTA CHEESE

1 CUP (120 G) CONFECTIONERS' SUGAR

1 CUP (230 G) SOFTENED CREAM CHEESE

1 TEASPOON (5 ML) VANILLA EXTRACT

1 TEASPOON VERY FINELY GROUND ESPRESSO COFFEE BEANS

1 CUP (175 G) SEMI-SWEET CHOCOLATE CHIPS, DIVIDED

DIRECTIONS

Preheat the oven to 350°F (180°C, or gas mark 4). Line 2 large baking sheets with parchment paper.

TO MAKE THE COOKIES:

In a large bowl, with an electric mixer set at medium speed, beat the butter, granulated sugar, and brown sugar for 2 to 3 minutes, or until light and fluffy. Beat in the egg, coffee, and vanilla.

In a separate bowl, whisk the flour, oats, baking soda, cinnamon, nutmeg, cloves, and salt. Add the flour mixture to the creamed mixture and beat at medium speed until well combined.

Using a small scoop, form 12 to 16 cookies from the dough. Place them on the prepared sheets. Bake for about 10 minutes, or until golden brown and beginning to set. Remove from the oven and, after about 5 minutes, transfer the cookies to a rack to cool completely.

TO MAKE THE CANNOLI CREAM FILLING:

In a large bowl, with an electric mixer set at low speed, beat the ricotta, confectioners' sugar, cream cheese, and vanilla. Stir in the ground espresso and ½ cup (88 g) chocolate chips.

Make sandwiches with the cookies and the cannoli cream filling. Press a few of the remaining chocolate chips into the filling around the sides of the cookies as a garnish.

TIP: REFRIGERATE LEFTOVER COOKIES, AS THE FILLING IS PERISHABLE. THESE MAKE A DELICIOUS DESSERT TO BRING TO A PARTY. THE OATMEAL COOKIES ARE VERY GOOD WITHOUT THE FILLING AS WELL.

Rohan Marley

The founder of Marley Coffee and the son of legendary musician Bob Marley, Rohan Marley was born on the island of Jamaica. He moved to the United States and studied sociology at the University of Miami. There, he played for the Hurricanes football team as a linebacker before moving on to play football professionally for the Canadian Football League's Ottawa Rough Riders. Not long after starting his professional football career, Rohan decided to follow his father's longtime dream of becoming a farmer. He bought fifty-two acres of farmland in Jamaica's Blue Mountains in 1999, and in 2007, he founded Marley Coffee. In addition to running his coffee company, Rohan, who is a supporter of sustainable, organic, and fairly-traded farming practices, is an ambassador to Water Wise Coffee Project, which works to improve water access, protection, and cleanliness in coffee-producing countries around the world. Rohan is committed to continuing his father's dream of spreading "One Love" to the world.

ACKNOWLEDGMENTS

I would like to say thank you to everyone who helped make this project happen.

Rosemary Black, thanks for your hard work.

Stacey Glick, thank you for making the Marley Coffee and Chef Max collaboration happen.

To the Quarry Books team: You are all great. Love all the hard work you all put into this project.

Chef Max—glad you thought outside the box and made it happen. I never thought coffee and food would pair like it has.

The Marley Coffee Team: Wow! Thanks so much for supporting the vision and the brand.

James Hennessy, thanks for all your help in moving this along in the process. I truly appreciate you!!

Maxcel Hardy III

Chef Maxcel Hardy III, one of the leading chefs of his generation, fell in love with cooking while a student in the culinary arts program at Wharton High School in Tampa, Florida. Deciding he wanted a career in the culinary arts, he enrolled in the Miami campus of the esteemed Johnson and Wales University, from which he graduated, and then began to work as a personal chef. Through his company, Chef Max Miami, he has counted among his clients a roster of celebrities, including the Prince of Dubai and the Prime Minister of Turks and Caicos. Amar'e Stoudemire, the NBA All-Star, hired Max to be his fulltime personal chef in New York City. During the five years he cooked for Amar'e and his family, Max co-authored *Cooking with Amar'e: 100 Easy Recipes for Pros and Rookies in the Kitchen.*

As a competitor on Food Network's hit shows *Chopped* and *Beat Bobby Flay*, Max became well-known to TV viewers. Among many other TV shows, he also has appeared on Fox 5's *Good Day New York* and WABC News.

A philanthropist and the founder of One Chef Can 86 Hunger Foundation, a not-for-profit organization that works to raise awareness of the hunger epidemic in the United Sates, Chef Max also served for many years on the Culinary Council for Food Bank For New York City. Max travels around the globe leading youth seminars and cooking for the less fortunate. He recently traveled to Kenya to prepare meals at a local orphanage, and on a mission trip to Nevis in the West Indies, he prepared 400 meals for local residents. Max also is the creator of Chef Max Designs, a line of chef's apparel that puts a modern style on classic chef uniforms. Recently, Max relocated to Detroit, Michigan, his birthplace, and opened a restaurant called COOP.

ACKNOWLEDGMENTS

Creating this book has been a long labor of love and creating 100 amazing coffee recipes was challenging. I did not want this book to be just another cookbook sitting on the shelf. I wanted to create an experience for both coffee and non-coffee drinkers alike. I am grateful to each person who made this project a reality and to everyone who has supported me along the way.

To my loving daughter, Tenara Hardy, thank you for being such a sweetheart and Daddy's constant cheerleader, even when you say, "Daddy, that was only okay."

To my mom, thanks for always supporting me, especially during the writing of this book at a challenging time for me.

To my loving family—the Hardys and the Arnetts—you all are the best support system anyone can ask for. If it wasn't for our family chats, I would not have been able to laugh at 2 a.m. while writing.

To Stacey Glick, thank you for staying persistent and finding us the right deal. Lord knows it was tough.

To Rosemary Black, you are amazing. This one was tough but we made it happen. Thanks for your expertise, strategy, and your vision in helping us create this cookbook.

To Rohan Marley, man, I think back to the first time we met at B&B Burger with Amar'e Stoudemire—fast-forward a year when I called and said let's meet and do something with coffee—not knowing we would be working on a cookbook just a few months later.

To AM Media Group, Americk, Nick, Johnny, Comfort, you all are amazing. Thank you for making my food look amazing. Thanks for your creative eye. Love you guys. Who would have thought Book Number Two!?

To my Blujeen family, thank you Lance for allowing me to shoot in your beautiful restaurant. You and your team are amazing.

To my Food Bank For New York family and my Community Kitchen family, thanks for allowing me to shoot this project in the kitchen.

To Chef Lady Lex and Mom, you all did an amazing job with the dessert recipes. Thanks so much for your support.

Lindsay Brockington: I'm truly honored to have you part of this book. It was so much fun testing the drink recipes—well, you creating them and me tasting them! Thank you so much!

To Chef Sherri and Chef Juicy—wow! You all have truly made this process smooth. Thank you both for supporting me and listening to me scream and sing Anthony Hamilton and Maze in the kitchen every day.

To the Quarry Books family and Jonathan Simcosky, thank you for believing in this project and making this book a reality. Thank you to everyone involved with this project. Thank you for your expertise, strategy, and vision and for helping create this cookbook.

To my Harlem Haberdashery family, thank you for keeping my chef jackets on point, for allowing me to shoot a few shots in your beautiful boutique, and to my pal, Louis Johnson, my personal stylist. You are amazing. Thanks for our one-hour session after shoots!

Rosemary Black

The longtime food editor of the *New York Daily News*, Rosemary has been a senior editor at *Everyday Health*, where she produced articles on food, nutrition, and health. Rosemary has also been the food editor of *Dash*, a monthly cooking magazine from *Parade* magazine. She is the author of five cookbooks and writes about food for a variety of publications.

ACKNOWLEDGMENTS

A huge thanks to Chef Max and to Rohan for the opportunity to create this book with you, and to my agent, Stacey Glick, and my editor at Quarry Books, Jonathan Simcosky, for believing in this project right from the start. And to our wonderful copy editor, Mary Cassells, and to everyone at Quarry Books, especially Anne Re and Meredith Quinn. It's been a joy and a pleasure to work with all of you.

Index